THE
LEADERSHIP
CONTRACT

FIELD GUIDE

THE PERSONAL ROADMAP TO BECOMING
A TRULY ACCOUNTABLE LEADER

VINCE MOLINARO

WILEY

Published by John Wiley & Sons, Inc., Hoboken, New Jersey.
Published simultaneously in Canada.

Library of Congress Cataloging-in-Publication Data:

Names: Molinaro, Vince, author.
Title: The leadership contract field guide: the personal roadmap to becoming
  a truly accountable leader / by Vince Molinaro.
Description: Hoboken, New Jersey: John Wiley & Sons, Inc., [2018] | Includes index. |
Identifiers: LCCN 2017041398 (print) | LCCN 2017048580 (ebook) | ISBN 9781119440635 (epub) |
  ISBN 9781119440642 (pdf) | ISBN 9781119440659 (pbk.)
Subjects: LCSH: Leadership. | Organizational change.
Classification: LCC HD57.7 (ebook) | LCC HD57.7 .M6349 2018 (print) | DDC 658.4/092—dc23

Printed in the United States of America

10 9 8 7 6 5 4 3 2 1

This book is dedicated to my clients and colleagues. It has been an honor and a privilege to work with so many of you over my career. You have inspired me, challenged me, and taught me so much. Thank you!

Contents

Contents

Introduction: Let's Get Started

Welcome. This field guide is a companion to my book *The Leadership Contract* (third edition). The two books work hand in hand; the first provides you with the key concepts and ideas, while this field guide presents a set of practical and thought-provoking activities to help you take your leadership to a higher level of effectiveness. As you work through this field guide, you will find yourself stepping up in significant ways in your leadership role. You will become the truly accountable leader that your organization needs.

Before you can become a truly accountable leader and redefine how you lead, I believe every leader needs to pause and reflect on the questions that follow.

 Activity I.1: Pause and Reflect on Your Current Leadership Role

 20 to 30 minutes to complete

Find a pen or pencil. Write your answers in the space provided for each of the following questions. I will ask you to come back to these questions in the last chapter of this field guide.

1. What does it mean for you to be a leader today?

_____

_____

_____

2. What has shaped you to be the leader you are today?

_____

_____

_____

_____

_____

_____

3. What is your primary obligation as a leader?

_____

_____

_____

_____

_____

_____

_____

4. How is your success as a leader being impeded because you are avoiding some difficult things that you know you must do (for example, managing a poor performer or having a tough conversation with a colleague), but haven't done? Be honest with yourself.

_____

_____

_____

_____

_____

5. To what extent do you have trusting and mutually supportive relationships with peers and colleagues at work? How accountable have you been to maintain these relationships?

_____

_____

_____

_____

_____

_____

_____

How was that opening activity for you? For most of the leaders I've worked with, their typical response is, "This was hard" or "I've never really thought about these questions before."

I believe some leaders struggle with these questions mainly because they don't find enough time in their day-to-day roles to meaningfully pause and reflect on their leadership. Most of us in leadership roles are so consumed by our to-do lists, our projects, or hitting quarterly business results that we can lose touch with what it really means to be a truly accountable leader.

I have learned that if you want to be a truly accountable leader, then you have to start spending some time reflecting on what this means for you. That's what this field guide is all about: It is your personal road map to becoming a truly accountable leader.

The Purpose of This Field Guide

In *The Leadership Contract*, I shared a great quote from John W. Gardner—former Secretary of Health, Education, and Welfare under President Lyndon Johnson. He wrote extensively about leadership. In his book *On Leadership* (The Free Press, 1990), he said, "Accountability is as important as the concept of leadership. Those who are granted power must be held accountable."

I completely agree with Gardner's idea and believe that accountability is the bedrock of truly great leadership, so we will explore in this field guide what leadership accountability means and how you must bring it about in yourself. Every leader must do his or her part to step up and lead in a more accountable manner. At an individual level, this field guide will help you to:

- Understand the context in which you lead and identify the implications for how you must show up as an accountable leader.

- Explore ways to be a more deliberate, decisive, and purposeful leader.

- Identify your primary obligations as a truly accountable leader and be prepared to step up to meet these obligations.

- Resolve to tackle the hard work of leadership in a way that propels you, your team, and your organization forward.

- Build a stronger set of relationships and a real sense of community with your colleagues and fellow leaders so you can collectively lead your company into the future.

- Gain practical ways of sustaining your learning.

My sincere hope and wish for you is that by the end of our work together, you will come away with a clear sense of what you must do to be a truly accountable leader.

Leadership Accountability: The Critical Business Issue

Over the past five years, I've had the privilege to speak with leaders around the world about the ideas from *The Leadership Contract*. When the book first came out in 2013, I found that the core ideas immediately resonated with leaders. Leaders at all levels—from the front line to the C-suite—found meaning and practical value from the ideas. Then in January of 2016, the second edition of the book was released. I spent the next eighteen months traveling the world speaking with business leaders like you about leadership accountability.

It was clear to me, based on the hundreds of discussions, customer events, speeches, and presentations, that leadership accountability was a critical business issue. It was understandable, given the degree of change that was happening all around us. During my travels, I found there were unexpected changes of power in five of the world's top countries. Incumbent governments were ousted. What was particularly fascinating (or disturbing) was that no one saw it coming—especially not the political pollsters.

At the same time, many companies faced unprecedented disruption and uncertainty. Many leaders have been unable to adapt quickly enough to the change and ambiguity in their business environments.

I also learned through my travels that far too many political and corporate leaders continue to be embroiled in scandal and corruption. Every day, people are starting to express their frustration and disgust with ineffective leadership. They are demanding that corporate and political leaders be held to account.

Maybe this is why the ideas in *The Leadership Contract* are resonating so much. It is clear to me that we are at a point in our history when we desperately need real leadership accountability in our world, now more than ever. Unfortunately, it is also clear to me that there is a leadership accountability gap in many companies; our research has confirmed this (see Chapter 3 in *The Leadership Contract*).

This gap is even more significant because many organizations are at an inflection point—a period of change brought on by the need to develop a new business strategy, turn around chronic poor performance, or integrate different leadership cultures after a merger or acquisition. I have learned that at each of these inflection points, the expectations of leaders change—sometimes in dramatic ways. In every case, one fundamental theme is present: *Organizations need their leaders to step up and be truly accountable.*

The ideas in *The Leadership Contract* are the foundation for many companies looking to transform their leadership cultures. At the same time, many leaders have used the ideas to transform their own leadership at a personal level. These leaders have described the book to me as a "mindset" book—one that helps them really understand what it means to be a leader in today's world, and how to think more deeply about their leadership roles.

While the ideas in my book are helpful to many, the common feedback I receive is that my readers want more; they want to learn how to better apply the ideas at a personal and organizational level. That's why this field guide has been written.

A Description of This Field Guide

This field guide presents a road map to becoming a truly accountable leader. The book is organized into four sections as represented in the following image.

THE LEADERSHIP CONTRACT FIELD GUIDE
The Roadmap to Becoming a Truly Accountable Leader

SECTION ONE	SECTION TWO	SECTION THREE	SECTION FOUR
The Core Ideas	The Foundational Practices for Living the Leadership Contract	The Regular Practices for Living the Leadership Contract	The Turning Points of Leadership

1. What Is Leadership Accountability?
2. What Is the Leadership Contract?
3. Leadership Accountability in Action
4. The World in Which You Lead
5. Leadership Is a Decision — Make It
6. Leadership Is an Obligation — Step Up
7. Leadership Is Hard Work — Get Tough
8. Leadership Is a Community — Connect
9. Regular Practices for Living the Leadership Contract
10. Use the Turning Points of Leadership to Make Better Career Decisions

Section One: The Core Ideas

The chapters in this section summarize the key concepts from *The Leadership Contract* in an interactive manner. You will reflect on your own thoughts and ideas about leadership. Chapter 1 will explore leadership accountability. Chapter 2 will examine the four terms of the Leadership Contract. Chapter 3 will help you apply the ideas from Chapters 1 and 2 to a case example.

Section Two: The Foundational Practices for Living the Leadership Contract

The chapters in this section present what I refer to as foundational activities required to help you become a truly accountable leader. Leaders around the world have completed these activities as part of The Leadership Contract™ seminars and workshops. They have resonated well with leaders, and I'm sure you will gain valuable insights from completing them. I strongly encourage you to complete each of the activities in this section (this is why I call them "foundational"); they will help you realize positive benefits in your leadership role. Chapter 4 will show you how to better understand the context in which you lead and appreciate the expectations you will face as a leader. Chapters 5 to 8 are each devoted to exploring the foundational practices aligned to each of the four terms of the Leadership Contract.

Section Three: The Regular Practices for Living the Leadership Contract

Chapter 9 in this section presents what I refer to as the "regular" practices, which will help you translate and transfer the four terms into your leadership role. Activities are presented that you can complete on a daily, weekly, quarterly, and annual basis. You can review them all, and then pick the activities that will be most meaningful to you.

Section Four: The Turning Points of Leadership

This section concludes by revisiting the concepts of the turning points of leadership, which I first presented in *The Leadership Contract* book. It will provide insights and advice depending on whether you are new to leadership, in a front-line or mid-level role, or entering the executive ranks.

How to Use the Field Guide

As you glance through this field guide, you will find many valuable activities for you to complete and gain deeper insights into your own leadership accountability. It's important that you read about and know all of the core ideas from *The Leadership Contract*. I encourage you to read that book first. I will also ask you to refer back to that book as you complete the many activities in this field guide.

I would suggest you work through this field guide over time—meaning you will tackle a chapter, work through a few of the activities, and then come back to it after a period of time. The distance between your sessions will deepen your reflection and application of the many activities into your current leadership role.

You will find many varied activities in this field guide. Some you will do on your own. For others, I will ask you to reach out to others you work with. Some activities will take you anywhere from five to ten minutes to complete, while others will require sixty to ninety minutes. Each activity will have a suggested time required to complete it so you can gauge how much time you will need to set aside. To make it easier for you to follow along, the field guide includes a series of icons so you know what type of activity I will ask you to work on.

This icon is used when you are asked to read a section from *The Leadership Contract*.

 This icon is used when you are asked to complete an activity. This could involve providing your answers to a series of questions, completing a self-assessment survey or checklist, or reaching out to your peers and/or direct reports to receive feedback on your leadership.

 This icon is used after each activity, where I share additional reflections that I've gained when other leaders completed the same activity in our seminars, workshops, and leadership programs.

 This icon will provide additional suggestions for applying or using some of the activities from the chapter in other ways.

 This icon will indicate how much time the activity should take to complete.

Who Will Benefit from This Field Guide

This field guide has been written to appeal to many different people in a variety of leadership roles. This book will benefit anyone in a leadership role (at any level) who is keenly interested in becoming more accountable, or who wants to create a higher degree of leadership accountability in the organization. The activities will help leaders develop the mindset needed to be successful in their current or future leadership roles.

Let's look at how this book will be of value for leaders in different kinds of roles:

- **Individual Contributors.** More and more people who are not in formal leadership roles are being called upon to be leaders. You do not need direct reports to define yourself as a leader. The ideas in this field guide will help you gain the perspective to see yourself as more than an individual contributor and step up in more meaningful ways in your role.

- **Emerging Leaders.** If you are seen as an emerging leader in your organization, this field guide will help give you the insights you need to make the decision to start your leadership journey.

- **Front-Line Leaders.** If you are a new leader, or if this is your first time in a front-line team lead role, the ideas in this book will help you fast track and accelerate your growth and confidence as a leader.

- *Mid-Level Leaders.* If you are in a mid-level leadership role, this book will equip you with ideas and practical tools to help you drive change in your organization and manage the complexity of your role.

- *Executive-Level Leaders.* Finally, if you are in the executive ranks, the ideas in this book will help you become a more deliberate leader. This will help you set the right tone of accountability and be an example to the rest of the leaders in your organization.

In practice, we have also found the ideas in this field guide to be of benefit to the following additional audiences:

- Senior executives who need to transform their organizations and develop a new set of leadership expectations for their leaders. This field guide provides a way of thinking and an approach that we've successfully implemented with many clients.

- Human resources and talent management professionals—internal and external to an organization—interested in driving stronger leadership accountability at all levels.

- Leadership development and learning professionals looking for powerful ideas to embed in existing programs to help leaders become more accountable.

- Organization development and change management professionals looking for specific strategies to transform the leadership culture in their organizations.

- Members of the academic community interested in a practical text to teach their students about the changing role of leadership, and a complementary learning guide to an existing leadership curriculum or course.

- Students in MBA, organizational psychology, and human resources development programs interested in books that will support their understanding of how to be a more accountable leader.

- Management consultants seeking ideas and guidelines to provide advice to organizations on how to transform leadership to drive results.

- Executive coaches looking for proven activities to help their coaching clients gain greater insight into their leadership roles and develop the mindset needed to become more accountable day-to-day.

A Word of Warning

Now before you move ahead to the first chapter, I believe it's important for you to understand that the ideas and activities in this field guide are going to ask a lot of you.

As in *The Leadership Contract* book, there may be times when you feel overwhelmed by the ideas and activities in this field guide. You may feel they are completely unrealistic and possibly not worth doing.

You may not realize it but, at those moments, your own leadership accountability will be tested. You will know whether you have what it takes to be a truly accountable leader.

You will need to think hard about whether you are ready to commit to accepting the four terms of the Leadership Contract. If you come to realize that you are *not* ready to challenge yourself and hold yourself to account, you might want to put *The Leadership Contract* and this field guide back on the shelf for a while.

However, if you are ready to be all in and fully committed to becoming a truly accountable leader—one that your organization desperately needs you to be—then buckle down and get to work. I hope you will find this field guide a valuable tool to support your growth and development as a leader.

I encourage you to reach out at www.theleadershipcontract.com to share your story. There you'll also find my Gut Check for Leaders blogs, as well as additional insights and tools that will assist you in continuing your learning and growth. Good luck!

The Core Ideas

T his section of the book has three chapters that will summarize the key concepts of *The Leadership Contract*. You will explore these ideas in an interactive manner to help you personalize them for your own current leadership role.

THE LEADERSHIP CONTRACT FIELD GUIDE
The Roadmap to Becoming a Truly Accountable Leader

SECTION ONE	SECTION TWO	SECTION THREE	SECTION FOUR
The Core Ideas	The Foundational Practices for Living the Leadership Contract	The Regular Practices for Living the Leadership Contract	The Turning Points of Leadership

① **What Is Leadership Accountability?**
Learn what it takes to be a truly accountable leader

② **What Is the Leadership Contract?**
Explore the four terms of The Leadership Contract

③ **Leadership Accountability in Action**
Understand how accountable leaders show up

Chapter 1: What Is Leadership Accountability?

This chapter will help you understand what leadership accountability is and how you are currently demonstrating it in your role.

Chapter 2: What Is the Leadership Contract?

This chapter provides a summary of *The Leadership Contract* and its four terms. You will also complete a Leadership Contract Self-Assessment.

Chapter 3: Leadership Accountability in Action

This chapter will help you deepen your learning regarding the ideas of leadership accountability and the four terms of the Leadership Contract. You will do this by reading the stories of two leaders who work in the same company. Your job will be to recommend one of them as a high-potential candidate for an executive development program.

Chapter 1

What Is Leadership Accountability?

T hink of a time when you and a group of close friends went to a new restaurant for dinner. You had great expectations for your evening because you had heard that the restaurant was terrific.

Unfortunately, your experience was not at all terrific. It was average at best.

At the end of the meal, you and your friends were disappointed. In fact, many felt resentful for spending all that money. Now imagine it's a few days later and you are asked by another friend about your night out. You probably would say that the restaurant was mediocre at best. Not a great endorsement at all.

Webster's Dictionary defines the word "mediocre" as something of low quality, value, ability, or performance. Essentially, it's seen as something that is simply not good. That's exactly what that restaurant was: mediocre.

Most of us can cite other examples in life when we were left disappointed by a mediocre experience—a poor dining experience like I just described, a bad movie, or substandard service while shopping. These experiences leave us frustrated and, at times, even angry.

But you know what? We also have similar experiences in our working lives, especially when we have to work with leaders we describe as being mediocre.

Mediocre Leadership and Its Impact

One of the sad realities I've encountered as I speak with people from different parts of the world is how many of them share stories of working for bad bosses and mediocre leaders. It's astonishing how frequently the topic comes up once people know the kind of work that I do as a leadership adviser. As these people share their stories, they do so with the same emotional reactions: disappointment, disgust, and even outright anger. It's no wonder so many movies and television shows are based on stories of bad bosses and mediocre managers. Unfortunately, these experiences are far too common for most of us.

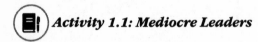

Activity 1.1: Mediocre Leaders

🕐 **5 minutes to complete**

Take a moment to think about your own experience with bad bosses or mediocre leaders. In the following space, write down what specifically these individuals did and did not do. Make sure you also capture how they made you feel.

_____

_____

_____

_____

_____

_____

_____

_____

Based on all my conversations, here are the most common themes that emerged from all the stories people shared about their experiences with mediocre leaders and bad bosses:

1. **Inept.** These leaders simply don't have the right instincts for leadership. They make bad (and even stupid) decisions that leave a trail of disaster behind. The worst ones are those who are incompetent but think they are great. No one can understand how these people were ever able to be put into a leadership role in the first place.

2. **Cowards.** They do not have the stomach for leadership. They always take the easy way out. They avoid difficult things. They don't take a stand, and they don't have a backbone.

3. **Lack of initiative.** They don't act. They're lazy and don't work hard. They look for the easy way out of any situation. They deflect responsibility or they always play under the radar, never to be seen or heard.

4. **Immature.** Even though they are adults, they typically act like temperamental toddlers. They have the emotional maturity of a two-year-old: When they don't get their way, they have temper tantrums. They can't handle any feedback; they become defensive and react with drama.

5. **Selfish.** They are only in it for themselves, taking as much as they can along the way. They have a huge sense of entitlement. They don't seem to care about the company they lead, the employees, or the customers. It's always about "ME, ME, ME!"

6. **Blame others.** When things go wrong, the finger always points at someone else. They never personally acknowledge their role or contribution if anything goes wrong.

7. **Highly insecure.** They lack confidence for the job, and this drives everything about who they are and what they do. They don't trust others. They surround themselves with weak or incompetent people. They stir the pot on teams by engaging in gossip. They, in turn, create teams that are insecure.

8. **Uncivil.** They regularly and routinely mistreat, disrespect, and insult others. They frequently "tear a strip off" their direct reports—often in public. They are bullies.

9. **Need to be liked.** They want to be your best friend and confuse the need to be liked with the need to be respected. They agree with everyone and everything. They avoid conflict or any confrontation. They never make an unpopular decision.

10. **Make excuses.** There is always a reason why something didn't work, and that reason never includes them. They never truly own the outcome of any situation.

Just writing this list makes me sick to my stomach. But that's how mediocre leaders and bad bosses make us feel. They demotivate, demoralize, and deflate your ambitions. They stifle your motivation. They can eliminate any desire to contribute in meaningful ways to your organization. The really bad bosses and truly mediocre ones demonstrate many of the items on this list. That's what makes them so ineffective.

The unfortunate reality for many people is that they can cite more examples of working with these types of leaders rather than examples of working with truly accountable and great leaders. In fact, I was asked by a leading national newspaper to submit an article on mediocre leaders that ran in their business section. The business section editor told me my article was one of the most popular that they had ever published and that it generated extremely high activity on social media. We can all relate to the experience of working with mediocre leaders.

So why did I begin this chapter by focusing on mediocre leaders and bad bosses? Quite simply because we cannot talk about truly accountable leadership without first appreciating what the absolute opposite looks like.

We have to change this reality in our organizations and in ourselves. Why is this so important? Because being a leader today is a very different proposition than it was a generation ago. When I first started my career, the model of leadership was very different. The world was a simpler place. You could have one or two leaders at the top of the hierarchy who knew their industry well and could create the strategy for success. All the remaining managers and leaders needed to simply carry out the orders from above and do their jobs. I worked with and saw many of these mediocre managers. However, it didn't seem to matter because there was leadership strength at the top. This model actually worked for a long time.

Today, we live and work in a very different world—one that is much more complex, uncertain, and ambiguous than perhaps at any time in our history. Many companies find themselves at critical inflection points, unsure of how to remain viable and drive sustainable growth. Yesterday's model of leadership is not effective for today's world.

Strong and accountable leadership is more important now than ever before, and it's required at every level in an organization. When you work with a leader who is truly an accountable leader, your experience is completely different from what we described previously. When you work with an accountable leader, you give everything you have. You are fully engaged and committed. You want to emulate the leader and do what is necessary to help him or her be successful.

This is why I believe the ideas in *The Leadership Contract* have resonated so well with organizations and their leaders. It's time to stop settling and tolerating mediocrity from our leaders. We need leaders to be truly accountable.

But before we continue, I have one more question for you in this section. I have found that it's easy for people to talk about mediocre leaders and bad bosses when they are referring to others. I find that we are much more uncomfortable looking in the mirror and admitting that, quite possibly, we may be mediocre ourselves. So here's the next question for you.

 ### Activity 1.2: Are You a Mediocre Leader?

 5 minutes to complete

How many of the ten characteristics previously listed do you demonstrate (or have demonstrated in the past) in your leadership role? What impact has this had on your capacity to be an accountable leader?

_____

_____

_____

_____

_____

Reflections

It's important for you to be honest with yourself. I suspect that, for many of you, the answer you wrote down wasn't one you are happy with. I was in The Netherlands, in the city of Eindhoven, speaking to a group of senior executives. During a question-and-answer period, a CEO spoke up. He said that as he reflected on the ideas I was sharing, he realized that he had allowed himself to become mediocre. He wasn't even aware of how it happened. He shared that he had begun to settle and accept mediocrity in himself and the leaders in his company. That insight shocked him.

I believe his story is fairly typical. Many mediocre leaders do not start out that way; but once you start settling, even in very small ways, then you find yourself on a slippery slope. Before you know it, you become like this CEO. At least he had the courage to look at himself in the mirror and challenge his own leadership. This field guide will, I hope, help you do the same. If we are to be truly accountable leaders, the first important step is to make sure we don't settle; we don't tolerate mediocrity in ourselves or others. We continually set high standards personally and for our teams.

Now let's shift our focus and explore what real leadership accountability is and what it looks like in action.

Leadership Accountability

Earlier in this field guide, I referenced the global research we conducted on leadership accountability. You can go back to Chapter 3 in *The Leadership Contract* to review the findings. One of the most interesting results that we discovered was the list of five critical behaviors that truly accountable leaders demonstrate every single day. These five behaviors surface whether the company is an industry-leading, high-performing one, or an average or below average performer. These five behaviors were consistently demonstrated across all the companies completing our survey globally. In other words, truly accountable leaders demonstrate very similar behaviors, regardless of the type of company or geography. Here are the five behaviors of truly accountable leaders (see Figure 1.1).

1 Holding others accountable for high
standards of performance

2 Tackling tough issues and making
difficult decisions

3 Effectively communicating the strategy
throughout the organization

4 Expressing optimism about the company
and its future

5 Displaying clarity about external trends
in the business environment

Figure 1.1 The Top Five Behaviors of Truly Accountable Leaders

Activity 1.3: Review The Top Five Behaviors of Truly Accountable Leaders

15 minutes to complete

Assess your own leadership against these five behaviors. To what extent do you truly hold others accountable for high standards of performance?

_____

_____

To what extent do you consistently tackle tough issues and make difficult decisions as a leader?

_____

_____

To what extent do you effectively communicate the organization's strategy to your team?

_____

_____

To what extent do you express optimism about the company and its future?

_____

_____

To what extent do you display clarity about external trends in your business environment?

_____

_____

Now let's explore specifically what I mean by "leadership accountability." Based on my research and extensive client work, my definition of leadership accountability has three parts.

First, leadership accountability happens when leaders take complete ownership for their entire role—both the technical and people aspects of the job. Every leader is being asked to drive business results. That's a given. But you are also being asked to develop teams, address poor performers, and create a compelling work environment and culture. When you own your entire leadership role, you embrace all parts of the job. My team and I have learned that many leaders miss this first part of the definition. Those leaders are in a leadership role, but they really only pay attention to the technical or functional parts of their jobs. They either deemphasize or completely ignore the broader leadership expect-ations of their roles. They are, in many ways, only part-time leaders. In other words, they only pay attention to a small part of their broader role and expectations.

Activity 1.4: Do You Own Your Entire Leadership Role?

⏱ **15 to 20 minutes to complete all activities in this section**

To what extent do you own your entire leadership role? Explain your response.

_____

_____

_____

_____

Second, leadership accountability is demonstrated when a leader acts in a deliberate and decisive manner. You must be clear about your responsibilities and commit to fulfilling them every day. In my experience, few leaders bring a high level of clarity, deliberateness, and decisiveness to their roles. Even fewer leaders can tell you, with any degree of confidence, what guides their leadership, the values that anchor them, or their personal visions for themselves as leaders. Are you one of these leaders?

Activity 1.5: Are You a Deliberate and Decisive Leader?

Would others describe you as being a decisive and deliberate leader? Explain your response.

_____

_____

_____

Finally, leadership accountability is demonstrated when leaders bring a sense of urgency to their entire leadership role; they tackle tough issues when they arise and rarely shy away from a challenge. They are focused on ensuring their organization is always moving forward and growing stronger every day. You must bring a sense of urgency to the important and difficult tasks that you have a tendency to avoid. When you avoid these tasks, you weaken your organization; it stagnates, gets stuck, and doesn't move forward. The key I find is not to bring a sense of frenetic or mindless urgency, but to really be mindful on driving priorities forward. My team and I see too many leaders who are either passively waiting for permission or hoping things will get better. If this is you, then you are not bringing enough urgency to your role as a leader.

 Activity 1.6: Do You Bring a Sense of Urgency to Your Entire Leadership Role?

How do you bring a sense of urgency to your entire role as a leader to tackle the tough issues in a way that makes your organization stronger?

_____

_____

_____

_____

_____

_____

_____

Reflections

What did you learn about yourself as you reflected on the three parts of the definition of leadership accountability? Few leaders can say that they can answer each question with complete confidence; we all have personal gaps in demonstrating real leadership accountability.

Let's face it: Many leaders struggle to fulfill the accountabilities of their leadership roles. Some focus more on the technical parts of their roles and make leadership a part-time portion of their jobs.

Most leaders see much more opportunity to lead in a more deliberate and decisive manner. Often, they do not have a clear sense of the kind of leader they need to be, and this limits them. Or they have a tendency to wait for permission—waiting for others to be decisive. Some feel they are not empowered to be decisive, as they do not have real decision-making authority in their companies.

Most leaders conclude that they can, in fact, do a much better job of bringing more urgency to important—but often avoided—tasks in their role. Leaders can often easily identify many areas that they have been avoiding, delaying, or addressing with only partial commitment.

What is also important to understand is that all three parts of this definition must be present for real leadership accountability to exist. For example, if you believe you own your entire role and that you are deliberate and decisive, but you do not bring a sense of urgency to your role, then you aren't a truly accountable leader. All three parts must be present and working together in an integrated way as you lead.

Final Thoughts

This chapter introduced and helped you understand the concept of leadership accountability. In the next chapter, we explore the four terms of the Leadership Contract because they provide the road map to help you become the truly accountable leader your organization needs.

Chapter 2

What Is the Leadership Contract?

I believe it is human nature to hold anyone we deem "a leader" to a higher standard of behavior. It doesn't matter whether that person is the head of a country, a CEO of a company, an executive, a senior manager, a front-line supervisor, or a team lead. Once we know that people are in a leadership role, we expect more from them. We always have high expectations of our leaders—and so we should.

As a result, when you take on a leadership role, you are signing up for something really important. You are being held to a higher standard of behavior and expectations.

To me, this implies that there is a contract when you take on a leadership role at any level. This contract demands that you be clear on what it means to be a leader; you must understand the expectations people have of you. It also demands that you commit to leading in a truly accountable manner.

I believe this leadership contract has always existed, but it is more important today because being an accountable leader is more critical. This leadership contract isn't just for our most senior leaders; it applies to anyone in any leadership role.

Nonetheless, I find too many leaders are not entirely clear that a leadership contract even exists; many have not read its terms and conditions. Others simply click "agree" the way we do when we're completing online transactions. The window with the online contract pops up on our laptop screen or tablet, and then we quickly scroll to the bottom and click "agree." We never read the terms and conditions in any detail.

I have come to learn that far too many leaders have clicked "agree" to take on a leadership role. Now you may have done so for valid reasons—to receive a promotion, a higher salary, the perks, the power, or the opportunity to have a real impact. But if you don't fully appreciate what you have signed up for, you won't be effective in leading through the pressures of today's business environment. Becoming a truly accountable leader means you need to understand that a leadership contract does indeed exist and that it has four terms and conditions.

Activity 2.1: Understanding the Four Terms of the Leadership Contract

120 minutes to complete all the activities in this section

In this section, I'm going to ask you to review the core ideas within each term of the Leadership Contract. I will provide a quick summary of each of the four terms (see Figure 2.1), and then present a series of questions for you to reflect on and answer.

1. Leadership Is a Decision—Make It

Accountable leaders must make the deliberate decision to lead. You must set high expectations for your personal performance and for those whom you lead. This term

Figure 2.1 The Four Terms of the Leadership Contract

of the Leadership Contract demands that you make the personal commitment to be the best leader you can be—the truly accountable leader your company needs.

Review Chapter 5 in *The Leadership Contract* book and answer the following questions.

In your own words, what does Leadership Is a Decision—Make It mean to you?

_____

_____

_____

_____

What has been your experience with Big D leadership decisions? How would you rate your overall effectiveness and why?

_____

_____

_____

_____

_____

_____

What has been your experience with small d leadership decisions? How effective were you in making these small d leadership decisions and why?

_____

_____

_____

_____

2. Leadership Is an Obligation—Step Up

Once you have decided to lead, you will quickly learn you are going to be held to a higher standard. As an accountable leader, you must be clear about your core obligations to your customers, your employees, your organization, and the communities in which you do business. You must bring a "one company" perspective to your role and put what's best for the organization ahead of your own self-interest. You must commit every day to making a meaningful impact and leaving your organization a stronger place.

Review Chapter 6 in *The Leadership Contract* book and answer the following questions.

In your own words, what does Leadership Is an Obligation—Step Up mean to you?

_____

_____

_____

_____

To what extent have you and do you lead today with a clear sense of your leadership obligations?

_____

_____

_____

_____

_____

3. Leadership Is Hard Work—Get Tough

Being a leader is not easy. Well, it can be if you are satisfied with being a mediocre one. However, if you aspire to be truly accountable and possibly even a great leader, this will require considerable commitment. You need to be resilient and determined to tackle the hard work of leadership. You need personal resolve and tenacity to rise above the daily pressures to lead your organization into the future. This term of the Leadership Contract demands that you get tough and do the hard work that you must do as a leader.

Review Chapter 7 in *The Leadership Contract* book and answer the following questions.

In your own words, what does Leadership Is Hard Work—Get Tough mean to you in your own journey as a leader?

_____

_____

_____

_____

How would you describe the hard rule of leadership to a peer or colleague? What examples would you use to illustrate it?

_____

_____

_____

_____

_____

Describe how you must Get Tough and build increased resilience and resolve to be successful in your leadership role.

_____

_____

_____

_____

_____

_____

4. Leadership Is a Community—Connect

Today, we need to build a strong community of leaders. Imagine that you and your colleagues are all fully committed to being great leaders and focused on supporting one another to be better—this would set your organization apart. This term of the Leadership Contract demands that you connect with others to create a strong community of leaders within your organization—a community in which there is deep trust and support, you know everyone has your back, and all leaders share the collective aspiration to be truly accountable leaders.

Review Chapter 8 in *The Leadership Contract* book and answer the following questions.

In your own words, what does Leadership Is a Community—Connect mean to you? To what extent have you supported the creation of a community of leaders in your organization?

_____

_____

_____

_____

Describe your own experience working in an organization with a Rotting of Zombies culture, a League of Heroes culture, or a Stable of Thoroughbreds culture. What was the impact to the organization? What was your role—good and bad—in addressing this culture?

_____

_____

_____

_____

How would you describe to someone else what a strong community of leaders culture looks and feels like? What impact would this have on the leaders and employees of an organization?

_____

_____

_____

_____

_____

 Activity 2.2: The Leadership Contract Self-Assessment

 30 minutes to complete

Now that you understand what the four terms of the Leadership Contract mean, let's explore how they currently apply to you as a leader. Take a few minutes to complete The Leadership Contract Self-Assessment. It will give you a quick snapshot of your current level of leadership accountability. Rate yourself on each statement using a 5-point scale, with "1" representing Strongly Disagree and "5" representing Strongly Agree. Your answers will be tallied for each of the four sections at the end of the survey.

The Leadership Contract Self-Assessment Survey

	Not at All Like Me		Somewhat Like Me		Very Much Like Me
Leadership Is a Decision					
1. I have deliberately decided to be a leader in my organization.	①	②	③	④	⑤
2. I am clear on what is expected of me in my leadership role.	①	②	③	④	⑤
3. I fully embrace the challenges and difficulties that come with being a leader.	①	②	③	④	⑤
4. I am very excited about my leadership role.	①	②	③	④	⑤
5. I pay attention to how I show up as a leader each and every day.	①	②	③	④	⑤
Leadership Is an Obligation					
6. I am fully committed to being the best leader I can be.	①	②	③	④	⑤
7. I always put what is best for my organization ahead of what's best for me.	①	②	③	④	⑤
8. I actively work to leave my organization better than I found it.	①	②	③	④	⑤
9. I know what each of my stakeholders values and expects of me.	①	②	③	④	⑤
10. I am absolutely clear on my personal obligations as a leader.	①	②	③	④	⑤

What Is the Leadership Contract?

	Not at All Like Me		Somewhat Like Me		Very Much Like Me
Leadership Is Hard Work					
11. I effectively handle the pressures and scrutiny of my leadership role.	①	②	③	④	⑤
12. I view the challenges I face as a leader as opportunities to grow and develop.	①	②	③	④	⑤
13. I never avoid tough conversations with the people I work with.	①	②	③	④	⑤
14. I never shy away from making decisions that may be difficult or unpopular.	①	②	③	④	⑤
15. I continuously work on developing my resilience and resolve as a leader.	①	②	③	④	⑤
Leadership Is a Community					
16. I actively look for ways to collaborate with my peers across the organization.	①	②	③	④	⑤
17. I always lead with a "one-company" mindset.	①	②	③	④	⑤
18. I build high-trust relationships with my fellow leaders.	①	②	③	④	⑤
19. I have a core group of peers I believe always has my back.	①	②	③	④	⑤
20. I have colleagues I can go to for advice and support.	①	②	③	④	⑤

The Leadership Contract Field Guide

Once you have rated yourself on each question, add up the ratings and enter the total score for each of the sections here:

Leadership Is a Decision	
Leadership Is an Obligation	
Leadership Is Hard Work	
Leadership Is a Community	
Total Score	

Your total responses to your self-assessment will provide a snapshot of your current leadership accountability aligned to each of the four terms:

Score	Interpretation
80 to 100	You have the mindset of an accountable leader. Keep assessing yourself on a regular basis to ensure you live up to the four terms of the Leadership Contract.
60 to 79	You have the foundation to be a more accountable leader. However, there is room for you to improve and step up in your leadership role.
59 or below	There may be many factors preventing you from stepping up to your role as a leader. Take time to reflect on whether you are committed to being an accountable leader and whether a leadership role is right for you.

Once you have tallied your scores, answer the following questions.

What personal insights did you gain from completing The Leadership Contract Self-Assessment?

_____

_____

_____

_____

_____

_____

_____

_____

_____

_____

_____

What are your top two areas of strength?

_____

_____

_____

_____

_____

_____

_____

_____

_____

_____

What are two areas in which you need to be stronger? Keep these two areas of development top of mind as you continue to work through the other chapters of this field guide.

_____

_____

_____

_____

_____

_____

_____

_____

_____

_____

Reflections

When my team and I ask other leaders like you to complete The Leadership Contract Self-Assessment, several common themes emerge in our discussions.

First, many tell us that they have not thought about their roles in this way before. The four terms provide a thought-provoking and practical way to think about their roles. Many also say that the approach gives them structure that helps them to be more reflective and, in turn, more accountable.

Second, when people are truly honest with themselves, many admit that they never made the deliberate decision to define themselves as leaders. The most common reason they cite is that they became leaders almost by accident. They were very strong technical performers and individual contributors who were promoted into a supervisory role and jumped on the management track. They felt compelled to stay on that track because it often paid more money, had better titles, and people felt they could have more impact. These are all valid reasons, but not enough, in my opinion, to take on a leadership role. Since the demands and expectations are so great, it is critical that you pause and think about the deliberate decision to define yourself as an accountable leader.

Third, many also tell us that they rarely think about their roles from an obligation perspective. Many leaders have told me, "That's a pretty big word that carries a lot of weight!" They are absolutely right. You have to feel the weight of the obligations of your role. That's what it means to be a leader today. I've also learned that some react negatively to the word "obligation." They see the term meaning something they are *forced* to do. That's not really the perspective I take when using this word. It really comes from the reality that, as a leader, people expect a lot from you. As a result, you must lead in a way that creates value for those people, whether they are your employees, customers, or other stakeholders.

Fourth, the majority of leaders admit that they must do a better job of tackling the hard work in their roles. They cite many examples in which they are avoiding the difficult challenges they face or delay confronting these challenges as long as possible. Interestingly, these same leaders leave our programs with a renewed sense of commitment to tackle the hard work in their roles.

Finally, most leaders admit that they don't spend nearly as much time as they should building relationships with their colleagues. It's surprising to see how few believe that their colleagues have their backs and truly support them. To me, this is one of the greatest untapped and missed opportunities for leaders. When you lead, make sure you are building strong relationships with peers and colleagues; you'll see how it dramatically improves the quality of leadership across your entire organization.

 Activity 2.3: Sign the Leadership Contract

 15 minutes to complete

The last activity in this chapter requires you to sign the Leadership Contract. You must demonstrate your commitment to be a truly accountable leader before you can explore the remaining chapters of this field guide.

I have included a copy of the Leadership Contract that I presented in Chapter 9 of *The Leadership Contract*. Review it now and, if you agree with it, then sign it!

THE LEADERSHIP CONTRACT™

I understand that The Leadership Contract™ represents a deep and personal commitment to being the best leader that I can be—the leader my organization needs me to be. By signing The Leadership Contract™, I am making a personal commitment to myself. In turn, I will no longer settle for mediocrity. I will not simply go through the motions as a leader. I will be an accountable leader. I understand that I can choose to share my commitment with others, or I can keep it to myself. Either way, those around me will know that I've signed up for The Leadership Contract™ based on the way I show up each and every day as a leader.

1. Leadership Is a Decision—**Make It**
I understand that leadership is a decision, and by signing below, I decide to be a leader. This means that I will be aware of when I need to make Big D leadership decisions. I also will bring this clarity to my role each and every day as I make effective small d leadership decisions.

2. Leadership Is an Obligation—**Step Up**
I understand that I am obligated to be the best leader I can be. I have an obligation to my customers, my employees, my organization, and the communities in which we do business. I will lead in an ethical manner. I will live up to the position of responsibility that my organization has given me.

3. Leadership Is Hard Work—**Get Tough**
I understand that as a leader there is hard work that I must do to make my organization successful. I also understand that if I avoid the hard work, I will make myself, my team, and my organization weaker. I commit to not being a bystander or a spectator. I will demonstrate resilience and personal resolve to tackle the hard work.

4. Leadership Is a Community—**Connect**
I will work to create a strong community of leaders in my organization. I will aspire to great leadership in myself and encourage it in others. I will set the tone for other leaders. I will strive to be the leader whom others want to emulate. I will build relationships based on trust, respect, and mutual support. I will work to drive greater clarity and commitment among our leaders so that we can effectively execute our strategy and help make our organization successful.

I agree to the Four Terms of The Leadership Contract™ set out above and will demonstrate my commitment by signing below.

✗ _____ Date: _____

What Is the Leadership Contract?

Final Thoughts

Leadership matters more than ever. Your organization needs you to be the most accountable leader you can be. It's not acceptable to be a mediocre leader. It also is not good enough to be a good or an average leader. You can't make leadership just one aspect of your job, something you focus on only when you have a few minutes of spare time. You must make leadership your entire job. It's time to aspire to more. It's time for you to be a great leader—one who is truly accountable.

Chapter 3

Leadership Accountability in Action

I n the last two chapters, you had an opportunity to understand the term "leadership accountability" and to explore the four terms of the Leadership Contract. This chapter will allow you to bring all these ideas together and appreciate how strong leadership accountability shows up day to day.

Let me introduce two leaders: Tim and Annie. Both are plant managers for the same hydropower company.

Activity 3.1: The Talent Review Process—Your Recommendations

30 minutes to complete all activities in this section

As you complete this activity, I'm going to ask you to imagine that you are an executive at this hydropower company. In two months, you will be taking part in a talent review meeting. You have been specifically asked by your CEO and head of human resources to come to the talent review meeting prepared to provide your recommendation as to which of the two leaders should be identified as a high-potential candidate for your company's executive development program. This is a strategic talent development initiative to grow your company's future executive-level leaders. The leaders selected will go through a rigorous two-year development experience. The investment your company is making will be significant, so your recommendation matters.

To help you arrive at your recommendation, you will be provided with a brief background on each leader. You will also be asked to use the definition of "leadership accountability" and the four terms of the Leadership Contract to help you assess each leader and, in turn, make your recommendation during the talent review meeting.

Here's some additional context for you to consider. Both leaders have important roles running their hydropower plants, which operate 24/7 to churn out megawatts of electricity. From a technical perspective, Tim and Annie must manage power loads and production, establish a safety culture, and orchestrate daily, weekly, monthly, quarterly, and annual maintenance. However, as plant managers they also need to focus on the other aspects of leadership, such as leading plant staff, managing relationships with internal and external stakeholders, developing other leaders, and supporting the execution of corporate priorities within the plant environment. These are emerging expectations of all leaders in the hydropower company.

Now let's learn a little more about the specific background stories for both Tim and Annie. Read each one and complete the activity that follows each story.

Tim's Story

Tim manages about 300 employees, including a team of six production managers. He has a solid background in engineering and operations. Like many leaders, Tim rose through the ranks because of his technical skills and strength as an engineer. He loves being an engineer.

Tim's plant always hits its production quotas and meets safety expectations. He is very data-oriented, and he credits his success to the fact that he "knows his stuff."

Tim starts his day with an update meeting on plant operations. He gets the information he needs from his directors of operations and maintenance, as well as from his production managers. The meetings are usually a series of one-way discussions; Tim is the hub, and the others serve as the spokes. He also reads reports from the previous night's shift; they give him key stats on the plant's operation. His desk is usually piled high with papers. He's often heard saying, "I get everything I need to run this plant from these."

In his weekly team meetings with production managers, Tim is laser-focused on poring over data and flagging areas for improvement. When problems arise, Tim wants to solve them as quickly as possible, and he typically dictates the solution based on his vast experience. He believes his direct reports are good at their jobs, but they don't have the same experience that he does, so they can't see the answers the way he can. Tim really shines in a crisis. His team marvels at his ability to bring real focus and direction to the technical issues that must be addressed.

Tim is the face of his company in the local community, but he tends to avoid external events and functions. He believes he is serving his community by generating the power it needs.

Tim doesn't keep it a secret that he detests corporate initiatives, including what he calls "the latest harebrained policy from finance or fluffy HR programs." Tim largely ignores any communications from above; he wants his team focused on operations, not distracted by the "corporate noise." Throughout the company, Tim's plant is viewed as "Tim's world." Despite this, Tim is respected in the organization for his loyalty, long-standing tenure, and deep technical expertise.

Based on this brief background about Tim, answer these questions:

What do you believe are Tim's top two strengths as an accountable leader?

_____

_____

_____

Think about the four terms of the Leadership Contract; where do you believe Tim needs to be stronger as a leader?

_____

_____

_____

Annie's Story

Annie's plant has a similar number of production managers and employees, and she also has a solid engineering background. Like Tim, Annie is data-oriented but says that she knows her job is more than just numbers. "By the time I see bad numbers, it's too late for me to do something," Annie frequently tells people. "The numbers don't always tell the whole story."

So Annie frequently walks the plant, taking time to chat with production managers and front-line employees. Annie accepts that she is the face of the company in the community and spends time managing relationships with local groups (such as the Chamber of Commerce) and other stakeholders (small business associations and manufacturing companies). She sets time aside in her schedule to meet with them, either visiting them or having them come to the plant for tours. During the tours, she makes sure that employees have an opportunity to interact with these important visitors. She believes strongly that employees need to have a clear understanding of how their jobs affect the broader community.

Annie makes it a point to engage employees and union representatives to make sure she can defuse any issues before they become grievances. The chief union steward at Annie's plant will often drop into her office to discuss potential problems. The few grievances that have come up were dealt with respectfully. Annie is not afraid to tackle the most challenging people issues that may arise in her plant.

Annie is always looking for ways to understand the company's strategy and how different parts of the company can support one another. She has her production managers spend a small percentage of their time working on corporate initiatives. That's not expected from a plant, but Annie believes it's good business: "It helps my production managers see how their work contributes to the grand scheme of things. It also helps the plant, because the production managers make sure the programs coming from corporate make sense in the real world." Some of Annie's direct reports feel these initiatives can get in the way of their ability to focus on operational issues. Others also feel that Annie at times over-commits her team to priorities that may help the company overall, but have little impact to her plant's operations.

Her management team meetings focus on operational issues, but Annie also spends some time on strategic discussions. She doesn't dominate the conversation; she encourages her production managers to speak up, raise issues, and provide potential solutions. She believes it's important to run good, productive, engaging meetings and to set an example that her production managers can follow with their teams. Annie is also a big believer in direct communication with staff. She frequently holds small town hall meetings before employees begin their shifts to keep them abreast of corporate strategy, stakeholder expectations, and the plant's performance.

Annie is respected for her ability to build strong teams, drive collaboration and engagement in her plant, and stay connected with key stakeholders at the head office and in the community.

Based on this brief background about Annie, answer the following questions:

What do you believe are Annie's top two strengths as an accountable leader?

_____

_____

_____

_____

_____

_____

Think about the four terms of the Leadership Contract; where do you believe Annie needs to be stronger as a leader?

_____

_____

_____

_____

_____

 Activity 3.2: Who Is the Truly Accountable Leader?

 30 minutes to complete

In the following table, I would like you to compare and contrast Tim and Annie as leaders.

Specifically, think about how each leader demonstrates the four terms of the leadership contract. Write down your responses in the space provided.

Once you have completed your analysis, I will ask you to provide your recommendation as to whom you believe is the high-potential candidate for your organization's executive development program.

The Four Terms of the Leadership Contract	To what extent does Tim demonstrate this term in how he leads every day?	To what extent does Annie demonstrate this term in how she leads every day?
Leadership Is a Decision—Make It		
Leadership Is an Obligation—Step Up		
Leadership Is Hard Work—Get Tough		
Leadership Is a Community—Connect		

Leadership Accountability in Action

Activity 3.3: Your Final Recommendation

🕐 **15 minutes to complete**

Which leader will you put forth as a high-potential candidate for your company's executive development program? What led you to choose this leader?

_____

_____

_____

_____

_____

_____

_____

_____

_____

_____

_____

_____

_____

_____

Reflections

My team and I have done this activity many times with many different leaders in our seminars and leadership programs. I'm always fascinated by the level of dialogue and debate that emerges with the leaders in the sessions.

There is often widespread agreement that Tim focuses most of his energies on the technical aspects of his role. It makes sense: He gets paid to keep the lights on. There is also agreement that he does not step up to the broader leadership demands of his role. At the end of the day, this is where these two leaders diverge: Annie is seen as embracing her entire leadership role as she pays attention to both technical and broader leadership demands.

Now let's consider which leader is creating greater long-term value for the company. When I ask this question, some interesting responses are shared. While on the surface it appears that both leaders are driving strong performance in their plants, Annie is often seen as creating more value because she's building the capacity of her team, establishing better engagement among employees, building stronger relationships with key stakeholders inside and outside her plant, and serving as an ambassador for her company in the community.

Let's imagine for a moment that you were given the choice to work for Tim or Annie; whom would you choose? I've asked this question hundreds of times and the response is overwhelmingly in favor of Annie. Here are the most frequent reasons people share. First, as a member of Annie's team, you would receive a richer career and leadership experience, one filled with more opportunities for personal growth, challenge, and development. Second, you would feel that you were part of a real team that was having a real impact. Finally, you would feel that your leader would have your back and be someone who was always looking to support your success.

After all the debate and dialogue, leaders in our sessions most often recommend Annie to the high-potential development program. She is seen as a truly accountable leader who owns her entire leadership role. She is also seen as living up to the leadership expectations of her organizations. In the end, this is what organizations expect of all leaders today. This applies to you as well.

Like Annie, you have to demonstrate a high degree of deliberateness and decisiveness. You have to pay attention to bringing a sense of urgency to your role and address the challenges your organization faces so that it is always moving forward and becoming stronger.

 Activity 3.4: Leadership Accountability—Your Insights

 15 minutes to complete

What additional insights did you gain about your own leadership accountability as a result of completing this activity?

_____

_____

_____

_____

_____

_____

_____

If your organization was conducting a talent review process and selecting high-potentials based on their accountability, would *you* be picked? Why or why not? Explain your response.

_____

_____

_____

_____

_____

Final Thoughts

The first part of this field guide introduced you to the core ideas of *The Leadership Contract*. You first explored leadership accountability and the three parts of the definition. You then examined the four terms of the Leadership Contract. Finally, you had the opportunity to apply these ideas during a talent review process whereby leaders were evaluated based on the degree of leadership accountability that they demonstrated.

In the next part of this field guide, you will continue your journey on the road map by exploring the four terms of the Leadership Contract more thoroughly. I will ask you to complete a series of activities that represent the foundational practices that ensure you have a solid base from which to become a truly accountable leader.

The Foundational Practices for Living the Leadership Contract

I n *The Leadership Contract*, I describe a series of foundational activities to help leaders begin to pay attention to different things in their leadership roles—the things that will help them become truly accountable.

Thousands of leaders around the world have been exposed to these ideas through our Leadership Contract workshops and seminars. In this section, you will have the opportunity to complete these same activities.

THE LEADERSHIP CONTRACT FIELD GUIDE
The Roadmap to Becoming a Truly Accountable Leader

SECTION ONE	SECTION TWO	SECTION THREE	SECTION FOUR
The Core Ideas	The Foundational Practices for Living the Leadership Contract	The Regular Practices for Living the Leadership Contract	The Turning Points of Leadership

(4) **The World in Which You Lead**
Define your current and future context and identify what it means to you as a leader

(5) **Leadership Is a Decision — Make It**
Discover your personal leadership story and use it to inspire and connect with those you lead

(6) **Leadership Is an Obligation — Step Up**
Identify your primary value as a leader and create a compelling vision for yourself

(7) **Leadership Is Hard Work — Get Tough**
Set yourself apart as a leader by tackling the hard work that others avoid

(8) **Leadership Is a Community — Connect**
Create a strong leadership culture and be the leaders others want to follow

Chapter 4: The World in Which You Lead

This chapter will help you explore the context in which you are currently leading and appreciate how that context determines the ways in which you must step up as a leader.

Chapter 5: Leadership Is a Decision—Make It

This chapter will help you understand the experiences that have shaped you to be the leader you are today. Leaders in our sessions find that these insights help them become more deliberate and decisive in their roles.

Chapter 6: Leadership Is an Obligation—Step Up

This chapter will help you understand your primary obligation as a leader. We find that many of the leaders with whom we work do not have a good sense of this. The activities in this section will help you gain the clarity you need to step up in meaningful ways to create more enduring value for your organization, your customers, your employees, and other stakeholders.

Chapter 7: Leadership Is Hard Work—Get Tough

This chapter will help you understand the importance of getting tough and demonstrating the resolve to take on some of the difficult challenges you face in your role. Too often, leaders shy away from these challenges. This weakens them, their teams, and their organizations. In this chapter, you will learn how to develop the resolve and resilience to tackle the hard work of leadership.

Chapter 8: Leadership Is a Community—Connect

This chapter will help you build meaningful relationships with your peers and colleagues. Today, leadership in companies is much more networked and distributed. Strong relationships create the foundation for a robust leadership culture in your organization.

Chapter 4

The World in Which You Lead

A favorite quote of mine comes from Spanish philosopher José Ortega y Gasset, who once said, "Tell me what you pay attention to, and I'll tell you who you are." This quote applies directly to all of us in leadership roles. I've learned when working with leaders to ask what they pay attention to while they are leading. What I've gathered is that truly accountable leaders approach their roles differently; they pay attention to different things than less accountable ones do. I will come back to this theme later in the book; for now, I want you to think about what you pay attention to as a leader.

Here's a quick activity to start this chapter.

 Activity 4.1: Tell Me What You Pay Attention to

 10 minutes to complete

I'd like you to close your eyes and think about a typical week in your current leadership role. Consider all the activities, tasks, meetings, and projects that demand your time and energy. Got it? Great! Now I'd like you to answer the following question:

What do you spend most of your time paying attention to in your leadership role over the course of a week?

_____

_____

_____

Your answer to the question above tells me and others a lot about the kind of leader you are. When I ask leaders like you this question, it becomes clear that many leaders are consumed by operational issues; they are focused on delivering projects on time and driving results. Of course results are important, but the danger is that focusing too much on deadlines can make you too internally focused. When this happens, you find yourself focused on doing rather than leading. You also become cut off from the environment and the context in which you operate.

It's a common complaint from many leaders: "I'm too busy to find time to lead!" Does this describe you? As you completed the question above, did you find yourself focusing only on internal operational issues and challenges? If so, you are like most leaders out there.

In addition, senior executives I work with also express a desire and need to have leaders in their companies demonstrate a strong ability to think and behave more strategically. They are frustrated when they see their leaders too internally focused and disconnected from the business environment in which they lead.

It's time to change. Why? Because I've learned that it is a real challenge to be a truly accountable leader if you are not clear on your priorities. You need to understand the context in which you lead. This means having clarity about:

- The environment—the emerging trends and drivers that are impacting or will impact your organization

- The strategic imperatives of your organization

- The leadership expectations that your organization has of you and other leaders

Let's also go back and connect the dots for a moment to the global leadership accountability research I shared in Chapter 1. The findings clearly confirmed that two of the top five behaviors of truly accountability leaders are: their ability to have clarity about external trends in their business environment, and effectively communicate the organization's strategy to teams.

Therefore, this is why the first obligation of every leader is to gain clarity about the world in which he or she leads. Just as a company needs to scan its environment to anticipate emerging trends, spot opportunities, mitigate risks, and protect itself against threats, I believe individual leaders must do the same.

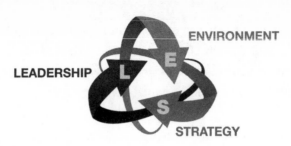

Figure 4.1 The E-S-L Model

But there's more. Not only do you need to have clarity around your context (your environment), you also need to understand what that context means for your business strategy (your strategy) and how you need to step up as a leader (your leadership). To help you achieve this clarity, I would like to introduce the E-S-L Model (see Figure 4.1): **E** stands for the environment in which you lead, **S** represents your company's strategy, and **L** represents leadership.

For the rest of this chapter, I will show you how you can use the E-S-L Model to develop a more holistic and strategic way of thinking about your leadership role. You will accomplish this by completing what I call a Leadership Context Map, and you'll come to realize the dynamic interplay that exists among these three variables.

First, you will consider your environment and identify the trends and drivers that are (or will be) impacting your organization over the next two to three years. Second, you will need to consider your organization's strategy and priorities. Third, you will think about the implications for you and your fellow leaders by identifying the leadership expectations and the pressures leaders will face. Finally, you'll consolidate your thinking and capture the main points on the Leadership Context Map worksheet (which essentially is a mind map that summarizes your key ideas on one page).

Before you start working on this activity, I'll share a completed sample so you are clear on what you will do.

Recall that in Chapter 3 I introduced you to Tim and Annie. Annie, being a truly accountable leader, took some time to think about her role using the E-S-L Model. She did her homework. She read her company's annual report and reviewed industry reports. She spoke to her direct manager and other colleagues to gain their perspectives.

She met with the company's head of strategy and corporate development. She found that her organization and the broader energy industry were extremely dynamic and ever-changing. Based on all this work, here is how she completed the Leadership Context Map:

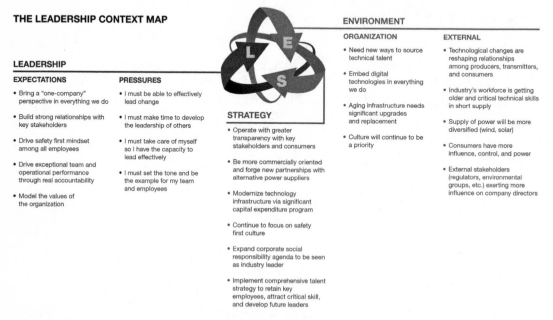

THE LEADERSHIP CONTEXT MAP

LEADERSHIP

EXPECTATIONS

- Bring a "one-company" perspective in everything we do
- Build strong relationships with key stakeholders
- Drive safety first mindset among all employees
- Drive exceptional team and operational performance through real accountability
- Model the values of the organization

PRESSURES

- I must be able to effectively lead change
- I must make time to develop the leadership of others
- I must take care of myself so I have the capacity to lead effectively
- I must set the tone and be the example for my team and employees

STRATEGY

- Operate with greater transparency with key stakeholders and consumers
- Be more commercially oriented and forge new partnerships with alternative power suppliers
- Modernize technology infrastructure via significant capital expenditure program
- Continue to focus on safety first culture
- Expand corporate social responsibility agenda to be seen as industry leader
- Implement comprehensive talent strategy to retain key employees, attract critical skill, and develop future leaders

ENVIRONMENT

ORGANIZATION

- Need new ways to source technical talent
- Embed digital technologies in everything we do
- Aging infrastructure needs significant upgrades and replacement
- Culture will continue to be a priority

EXTERNAL

- Technological changes are reshaping relationships among producers, transmitters, and consumers
- Industry's workforce is getting older and critical technical skills in short supply
- Supply of power will be more diversified (wind, solar)
- Consumers have more influence, control, and power
- External stakeholders (regulators, environmental groups, etc.) exerting more influence on company directors

Figure 4.2 Annie's Leadership Context Map

As you can see, Annie did a good job of capturing some of the larger macro trends in her environment. Based on her research, she learned about the six strategic priorities for her organization. While she already knew this information, this exercise had her internalize what these strategic priorities truly meant for her in her leadership role. With this insight, Annie then thought about and captured the leadership expectations for herself and other leaders.

The Leadership Context Map gives Annie a simple way to connect the dots among what is happening in her environment, the strategic priorities of her organization, and what she must pay attention to in order to be a truly accountable leader.

Activity 4.2: Apply the Leadership Context Map to Your Leadership Role

 45 to 60 minutes to complete all activities in this section

Begin by brainstorming your ideas. Then focus on the most critical points that require your attention as a leader. Finally, write those items on the Leadership Context Map. You can recreate the image on a separate sheet of paper. You can also download a template of the Leadership Context Map worksheet at www.theleadershipcontract.com.

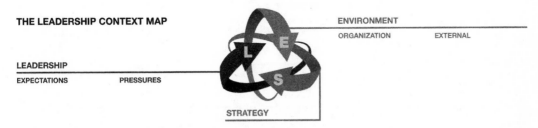

Figure 4.3 Your Leadership Context Map

Environment (E)

Macro trends. Think about your emerging environment over the next two to three years. Consider key trends and drivers happening in the world and capture the ones that will impact your organization the most. You might consider economic, political, technology, industry, regulatory, or societal issues. Write your brainstormed list in the following space.

_____

_____

_____

Industry trends. Now think about your emerging environment and identify what's happening within your industry. Think about trends with customers, technology, regulators, and other stakeholders. Write your brainstormed list in this space.

_____

_____

_____

_____

_____

Organizational issues. Now think about your organization and consider the big internal issues and challenges it will experience over the next three to five years. Will there be any challenges with your customers, supply of talent, engagement of employees, partners, and key stakeholders? Write your brainstormed list here.

_____

_____

_____

_____

_____

_____

Strategy (S)

Now consider the strategy of your organization. If you don't have an idea of what the strategy is (this is actually more common than you might think), you have some work to do. Meet with your manager or read your company's annual report. Or find time to talk to a colleague who has the insights you need. Once you have the information, reflect on the following:

List the strategic priorities of your organization in simple and clear language.

_____

_____

_____

_____

How do these strategic priorities translate and align to the priorities that you and your team are accountable to deliver?

_____

_____

_____

_____

_____

Leadership (L)

Now let's think about the last part of the Leadership Context Map—leadership.

Based on your understanding of your environment and your organization's strategic priorities, what do you believe are the expectations of all leaders?

_____

_____

_____

_____

Now consider the specific leadership expectations that you must live up to. Write them down.

_____

_____

_____

_____

_____

_____

_____

What pressures do these leadership expectations place on you?

_____

_____

_____

_____

How confident are you in your ability to meet these expectations?

_____

_____

_____

_____

Complete the Leadership Context Map

Review all of your insights from your work above and summarize the most critical points under each part by writing five to seven points each under Environment, Strategy, and Leadership on your map. Review the entire map, then answer the following question.

Given your context, in what specific ways will you need to step up to demonstrate strong leadership accountability?

_____

_____

_____

_____

Q Reflections

How difficult was it for you to complete this activity? Many leaders struggle with it the first time because it represents a new way of thinking about their leadership role. Here are some other patterns I've seen in working with other leaders like you.

First, it is still surprising to me how few leaders have a big-picture view of the world in which they lead. Part of the reason is that their jobs are so operationally focused that they find it difficult to pull themselves out of the weeds to think more broadly and more strategically. Don't let this happen to you.

Second, some leaders believe they don't have to worry about big macro trends. They believe that these are what only company executives should focus on. While there is some truth to this, the reality is that we need all leaders at all levels to bring a more strategic approach to their leadership roles. So force yourself every once in a while to pause and look at the world around you.

Third, it is surprising to see how few leaders have strategic clarity. Few can recite the strategic priorities of their organization. If you find yourself in this camp, you must change it. I don't know how anyone can be a truly accountable leader while living in the dark. Granted, some companies don't do a great job of explaining their strategic priorities to their leaders. But don't let this be a barrier to you. Do your homework. Talk to your manager. Read your company's annual report. The information is there; you just may have to work harder to find it.

Finally, few leaders have a good sense of their organization's leadership expectations. Recall the global research I shared in *The Leadership Contract*: Only 49 percent of companies we surveyed have even identified the leadership expectations for their leaders. This means there are a lot of leaders out there who are leading without a really good understanding of what their company expects them to do. Again, don't let this hold you back. Sit down with your manager and, at the very least, get clear on what he or she expects of you as a leader.

The Importance of Getting Clarity

You can't be a truly accountable leader if you do not have clarity—you must understand the context in which you lead. This means being clear about:

- The environment—the emerging trends and drivers that are impacting or will impact your organization—past, present, and future
- The strategic imperatives of your organization—current and future
- The leadership expectations that your organization has for you and other leaders—today and into the future

 ### *The E-S-L Model: Additional Uses*

The E-S-L Model is a practical and useful way to gain this level of clarity. Many leaders complete it on their own, but there are other practical uses for the E-S-L Model.

1. Prepare for Key Business Meetings. Refresh the Leadership Context Map every time you have a key business meeting with your manager or other senior leaders. By using the E-S-L Model, you'll be seen as a leader who brings a more holistic and strategic perspective on your organization while demonstrating a high degree of clarity and commitment.

2. Create Team Clarity. Consider doing the exercise you completed above with your own team. You will quickly see the value when team members can gain personal and collective clarity as to their context, strategy, and leadership expectations.

3. Redefine Leadership Expectations as Your Organization Evolves. It's important to come back to the E-S-L Model periodically, especially if your company has experienced a dramatic change triggered by an event in the operating environment or a significant change in business strategy. Typically, either of those changes (on their own or together) will cause you to revisit the leadership expectations you have for your leaders. If you do not do this, then leaders will be trying to lead in a new world with an old set of expectations.

4. Provide Context for Others. Many leaders with whom my team and I have worked say that the E-S-L Model has become a "mental device" that they use to effectively provide context for the people they lead. This is an important obligation for all leaders. The people you lead need to understand the big picture, how they fit in, and the expectations you have of them. Begin first by describing the environment, then ask them to connect the dots to the strategic priorities of their organization, and finally have them discuss the implications for what they pay attention to as leaders. Practice this right now. Pretend you are having a conversation with a key stakeholder outside your organization and complete the statements that follow. If you really want a challenge, take out your smartphone and capture a video of yourself responding to these questions. Look at it afterward to see how you show up as a leader. Or if you are not up to that challenge, simply write out what you will say after each caption shown in activity 4.3.

 Activity 4.3: Providing Context to the People You Lead

 20 minutes to complete

*I'd like to share with you how I'm thinking about our business and give you a sense of the context in which we are working. Here's what's happening in our **environment** and the key drivers we must pay attention to . . . .*

_____

_____

_____

_____

_____

_____

*If we are going to be successful, we must be able to execute against these **strategic priorities** . . . .*

_____

_____

_____

_____

_____

_____

*If we are all going to be **truly accountable as leaders**, it will be critical for us to . . . .*

_____

_____

_____

_____

_____

_____

In my own role, I will be paying attention to the following . . . .

_____

_____

_____

_____

_____

_____

_____

Final Thoughts

I began this chapter by asking you what you pay attention to as a leader. Review your initial answer. Given the work you did in this chapter with the E-S-L Model, how would you answer that question now? Go back and add some new insights.

If you are like most leaders, you might see that you have developed a more holistic and expanded view of what you should be paying attention to as a leader. This is important because we expect leaders always to have the big picture in mind rather than being consumed by daily tasks and operational issues. These things are important—but if that's all you are paying attention to, then you aren't really stepping up as a truly accountable leader.

With the E-S-L approach, you are now armed with a simple way of thinking about your leadership role, connecting the dots for yourself and the people you lead, and communicating with others about what you are trying to achieve.

You have done important work in this chapter. Congratulations!

Let's keep the momentum going as we start exploring the four terms of the Leadership Contract in the remaining chapters in this section of the field guide.

Chapter 5

Leadership Is a Decision—Make It

One of the very first questions I asked you to think about at the beginning of this field guide was: *What has shaped you to be the leader you are today?*

Take a minute right now to go back to the book's Introduction and review what you wrote.

When I ask leaders this question, many are surprised by it. Most don't have a good answer. But after they spend some time thinking about the question, ideas begin to emerge. In the end, most leaders realize how key experiences have played an important role in shaping them.

One of my favorite leadership thinkers, Warren Bennis, wrote in his book *On Becoming a Leader* that "Leaders, whatever their field, are made up as much of their experiences as their skills." His later research would reveal the importance of what he termed "crucible experiences"—defining moments that shape the way individuals think about their leadership and how they lead.

Unfortunately, few leaders are clear on how these important experiences and events in their lives have shaped them.

For example, consider that bad manager you may have worked for early in your career. What impact did he have on you? Or think about that truly great leader you worked for; what impact did she have on you? Recall a time when you faced a significant challenge at work that you somehow figured out how to overcome. What about a time when you may have failed? Or that peak career experience you may have had with a team when you delivered outstanding results?

Experiences like these leave their mark on each of us. Collectively, they tell a personal story of who you are as a leader. These experiences make us who we are, and they shape our mindsets, our beliefs about what it means to be a leader, how we make our decisions, and, ultimately, how we act as leaders every day.

But there's more. I have also learned that when you are able to gain clarity about how these experiences actually have influenced you, you start to become a more deliberate and intentional leader. This was my own experience when I first was introduced to this thinking early in my career. This is why understanding your personal leadership story is a foundational activity for the first term of the Leadership Contract, *Leadership Is a Decision—Make It* (see Figure 5.1).

By the end of this chapter, you will more clearly understand your own personal leadership story and learn how to share it effectively with those you work with and lead.

Figure 5.1 Leadership Is a Decision—Make It

Activity 5.1: Understanding Your Personal Leadership Story

 60 to 90 minutes to complete all the activities in this section

To successfully complete this activity, it's best to dedicate some uninterrupted quiet time. Here's what I will ask you to do:

- In Step 1, you will determine your critical leadership experiences. You will identify the experiences that you believe made you the leader you are today.

- In Step 2, you will map out your most critical leadership experiences along a timeline.

- In Step 3, I will ask you to examine the critical experiences that you mapped out on your timeline and identify the common themes and patterns that are core to your leadership story.

Step 1: Determine Your Critical Leadership Experiences

Below, I provide ten categories for you to consider as you begin to reflect on your life's leadership experiences. It is important to be as broad as possible in your thinking. Leadership does not just happen in organizations through formal leadership or managerial roles; leadership can happen at home, through volunteer positions, at school, through participation in sports, or in other life roles. That's why this activity gives you many different categories. You do not have to complete a response under each one, but they are there to stimulate broad thinking on your part.

Once you identify a critical experience, write it down by describing it in one or two sentences. Also capture in parentheses the time period during which the experience happened (the year). Here are a couple of examples:

- *I worked for Samuel, that difficult manager who was a horrendous boss. I eventually decided to leave the company as a result* (2014).

- *My team and I delivered the successful roll-out of a new product that was ahead of schedule and under budget. It helped our company capture market share from our key competitor* (2017).

Just remember that this is the brainstorming part of the activity. Capture as many critical and meaningful experiences as you can. As you start identifying your experiences, you will find more will come to mind. Capture as many as you can. Good luck!

1. Identify the important leadership experiences when you were the leader, manager, or supervisor of others.

_____

_____

_____

_____

_____

_____

2. Identify the key experiences of being led by a leader, manager, or supervisor (a great or a bad one).

_____

_____

_____

_____

_____

3. Identify the key family experiences or events when parents, siblings, and other relatives influenced you.

_____

_____

_____

_____

_____

_____

4. Identify experiences during your school years (elementary, high school, college/university) and/or the teachers and professors who had an impact on you.

_____

_____

_____

_____

_____

5. Identify spiritual/life experiences that influenced you.

_____

_____

_____

_____

_____

_____

6. Identify any important volunteer or community-based experiences that influenced you.

_____

_____

_____

_____

_____

7. Identify the key experiences you had through your participation in sports and other related activities.

_____

_____

_____

_____

_____

_____

8. Were there any historical individuals (such as business or political leaders, social activists, artists, or scientists) who influenced you?

_____

_____

_____

_____

_____

9. Are there important books that you've read or movies you've seen that influenced you?

_____

_____

_____

_____

_____

_____

10. Did you personally experience any significant economic or historical events (for example, the financial crisis of 2008) that influenced you?

_____

_____

_____

_____

_____

Step 2: Map Your Critical Experiences on Your Timeline

Review the list of experiences that you identified. Select those you believe have been most critical in shaping you as a leader; you are going to plot them on a timeline that looks like Figure 5.2. You can recreate this image on a separate sheet of paper. Or you can download a template of the Leadership Timeline worksheet at www.theleadershipcontract.com.

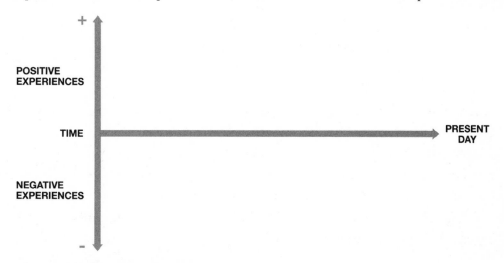

Figure 5.2 Leadership Timeline

As you can see, the horizontal line or axis represents the specific time when the experience took place. That's why I asked you to identify when your experience happened. The far right of the horizontal line represents today.

The vertical line or axis represents whether the experience was a positive or negative one for you at the time it happened.

If the experience was highly positive or a peak experience, you will plot it near the top of the vertical line on the timeline. If the experience was extremely negative (a low period), you will plot it near the bottom of the vertical line.

If the experience wasn't particularly low or high, you would plot it somewhere in the middle of the map.

Remember, it is important to plot the experience based on whether it was positive or negative in the moment. Sometimes when you look back at a negative experience, it may actually seem positive because the event triggered you to take some action that led you to a better outcome. But for the purpose of the activity, plot the experience based on what it

Leadership Is a Decision—Make It

felt like in the moment. Write down the year and a few words to describe the event or experience.

When I do this activity with groups, someone always asks, "How many experiences should I have?" The answer is that it depends. Clearly, the older you are the more opportunity you may have had to experience things. So you might have more experiences simply as a function of your age.

I find that most leaders will identify ten to fifteen key experiences that they map out during our session. If you end up having fewer than six, then perhaps you need to work a little harder at the activity. If you have more than twenty-five, then you might need to refine your list to make it more manageable.

Again, remember that this activity is intended to be meaningful for you. So do what makes sense and what will be most valuable for your own learning.

When you have mapped all of your experiences on your timeline, you might also find it interesting to create a line that connects each of the experiences. Then you immediately have a graph of your timeline that shows your highs and lows. Here is a sample completed timeline (Figure 5.3) from a leader named Elena who was a participant in one of our leadership development programs.

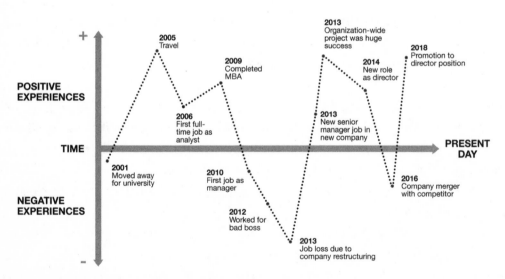

Figure 5.3 Elena's Leadership Timeline

Step 3: Identify Common Themes and Patterns

Once you've completed your timeline, by mapping out your critical experiences, look at it as a whole.

I'm sure as you reviewed Elena's timeline you immediately had a sense of her leadership story; the experiences that were extremely meaningful, both positive and negative. That's the value of mapping out your critical experiences: It gives you a way to see all of them on one page and see the connections and patterns across your leadership timeline.

I'm going to ask you to do the same analysis on your own leadership timeline. See whether your experiences connect with each other. Try to identify common patterns and themes.

Spend some focused time reviewing your leadership timeline and capturing your responses to the following reflective questions:

1. What common themes emerge across all of your leadership experiences?

_____

_____

_____

_____

_____

_____

_____

2. What differences do you notice between your positive and negative experiences?

_____

_____

_____

_____

_____

_____

3. When did you find yourself making a deliberate leadership decision (Big D or small d decisions)?

_____

_____

_____

_____

_____

4. When did you notice having a clear sense of your leadership obligations?

_____

_____

_____

_____

_____

_____

5. When were your personal resolve and resilience tested? How did you respond in the face of adversity?

_____

_____

_____

_____

_____

_____

6. Who played a critical role in your leadership timeline (to support or encourage you to be a better leader, or as a bad example of mediocre leadership)?

_____

_____

_____

_____

_____

_____

7. In what type of leadership cultures were you at your best as a leader? When were you not at your best?

_____

_____

_____

_____

_____

_____

8. What overall insights do you take away from this activity? How will it help you be more deliberate in the way you lead?

_____

_____

_____

_____

_____

_____

 Reflections

The leadership timeline activity that you just completed is very meaningful for many leaders. In the hundreds of sessions I've led during which leaders have completed their own leadership timelines, the vast majority have found it personally valuable.

One of the first insights that emerges is how valuable it is to pause and look back over one's career. Many leaders say, "I knew these experiences were important to me, but I didn't realize how much they influenced my current actions."

Others immediately gain a sense of personal clarity. We often hear, "I know the kind of leader I've been and the leader I now need to be." They feel energized by the insights they have gained.

Some leaders learn important things about themselves, including (at times) negative things related to how they treated others poorly in the past. Or they realize that they may have been a bully or tyrant as a leader. This doesn't sit well with them; however, acquiring this insight is valuable in many respects.

When exploring the patterns and themes across many timelines, some commonalities definitely emerge. For some leaders, a common theme is the influence of key people in their lives. Many can cite one or two individuals who have played important roles in shaping them. This often could be a parent or other important relative, a teacher, or the coach of a sports team. Former managers and mentors tend to come up a lot. What's interesting is that both great leaders and bad ones surface on the timelines. The bad ones teach us the kind of leader we don't want to be. The great ones are those we admire and still emulate to the present day.

Another common theme involves how adversity is handled. Those experiences that rate low on the vertical line tend to provide the greatest opportunities for personal learning. When you're struggling with something like the loss of a job, a failed project, or an unfulfilling career, you often learn a lesson in having the personal courage to confront a difficult circumstance. Looking back on tough experiences, people realize how fear got the better of them and paralyzed them from taking action in a bad situation. Many say, "I stayed much too long in that company or working for that jerk of a manager." Many leaders also realize that during really difficult times, they isolate themselves even further. Many admit being reluctant to ask for help, which in turn only makes dealing with difficult situations even harder.

The other really interesting pattern to emerge is that most peak experiences involve teams and working with others. Time and time again, we hear of the peak leadership experiences as not being solitary ones, but rather ones that were team-based or when leaders were part of a strong community. Conversely, many of the negative experiences are described as being lonely and solitary. This suggests the power of working with others and a sense of community (more on this in Chapter 8 of this field guide).

Leaders also come to appreciate the situations in which they have been most effective. For example, in my own story, I find I have been at my best as a leader when I've had a significant entrepreneurial challenge. I've learned that I'm a builder, not a maintainer. I don't tend to do as well in roles in which I must come in and keep things as they are. I don't maintain the status quo.

Knowing something like this about yourself becomes extremely valuable, especially as you look to assume future leadership roles. Your leadership timeline will tell you the situations, environment, and challenges that bring out the best in you. Leverage it as you make future leadership decisions.

Activity 5.2: Understanding Your Personal Leadership Story: Further Reflections

15 minutes to complete

Which of the common themes and patterns that I just shared in reflection section above ring true for you and why?

_____

_____

_____

_____

_____

_____

_____

Consider for a moment that your direct reports were completing their own leadership timeline maps. Where would you appear on their maps? Would you be above the line or below the line? What leads you to choose that place?

_____

_____

_____

_____

_____

As I already mentioned above, one of the key benefits of understanding your personal leadership story is that it brings personal clarity to who you are as a leader. This will help you be more deliberate and intentional as you lead into the future.

As you start encountering new challenges as a leader, you will find yourself pausing and thinking: "This experience is a new point on my leadership timeline." Just that thought will help you gain a valuable perspective on how you need to show up in that moment.

I also find that leaders who understand their leadership stories tend to better appreciate the first term of the Leadership Contract: *Leadership Is a Decision—Make It*. They also realize that this leadership decision isn't a one-time event. Rather, it happens many times over the course of their careers.

Share Your Leadership Story

Understanding what has shaped you to be the leader you are today helps to make you a more deliberate and intentional leader. Now you are clear on the leadership decisions you have made in the past; you have a greater appreciation of how you have handled success and failure. These insights and lessons will help as you take on future leadership roles. Many leaders find doing this type of personal reflection to be invaluable.

However, this represents only part of the work you must do. Your challenge is to make a commitment to share your personal leadership story with others. This will become a powerful way to connect with the people with whom you work and lead.

Dr. Nick Morgan, author of the successful book *Power Cues*, has written extensively on the power of stories and the role they play in effectively communicating with others. He believes that connecting with people is one of the highest forms of being for humans: "At the heart of it is good storytelling. Stories make us human."

This is why creating your personal leadership story is only one part of the equation. Now that you have it, you must share it with others. I've come to learn that it's one of the most powerful things any leader can do. Professor Noel Tichy wrote in his great book *The Leadership Engine* that leaders tell three stories:

- The who am I story (which you now know because of the work you have completed above);

- The who are we story (which describes the obligations you have as a leader and which you will explore in the next chapter); and

- The where we are going story (the work you completed in Chapter 4 helps you determine this story).

It is important to state right now that I know (from experience) that some of you will have no issues sharing your personal leadership stories with others. You are quite open and probably looking forward to doing so. I also know that others of you may be more tentative. You may be uncomfortable opening up and disclosing things about yourself. This is why I suggest a few basic ground rules to ensure success.

First, know that you own your personal story and share only what you are comfortable sharing. Second, tell your story from a place of humility. I've seen times when leaders spend all their time essentially bragging or only speaking about their positive and peak leadership experiences. I can always tell when this is going on during a leadership program because I can watch the body language of the participants. When someone is bragging, everyone simply tunes out.

When you tell your personal leadership story, be sincere and honest. I find people appreciate hearing stories of personal struggles more than those of success. In my experience, I find people are more keenly interested to learn how someone failed twenty times to achieve something once, not the other way around. When you do this, you immediately connect with people because you are confident enough to show your human side—your warts, struggles, failures, and of course a few successes. Some leaders are afraid of these moments. They think that they need to be eloquent, perfect, and flawless. Actually, the most critical thing to be is humble. Show your genuine human side.

It's Time to Share Your Personal Leadership Story

In order to tell your personal leadership story, you need to take your leadership timeline and begin making sense of it. Some leaders are able to just pull out the leadership timeline worksheet and tell their personal stories. Others want to take this important work to another level. This involves converting the leadership timeline into more of a narrative or written story.

 ### Activity 5.3: Creating a Narrative of Your Personal Leadership Story

 30 to 45 minutes to complete

If you are interested in creating a narrative of your personal leadership story, review Chapter 1 in *The Leadership Contract,* pages 1 through 19. This is where I shared my own personal leadership story. You can get a sense of how I approached mine.

In the end, you need to be clear on what the key experiences are—the ones that most impacted you as a leader—and write the story.

Review your leadership timeline and identify the key experiences you will include in your own narrative.

_____

_____

_____

_____

_____

_____

_____

Sharing Your Personal Leadership Story

Now that you have a clearer sense of the elements of your personal leadership story, take a moment to reflect on how you can share your leadership story with the people in your life. Here are some people to consider:

- **A Trusted Colleague or Mentor.** Share your personal leadership story with a trusted colleague or mentor to gain his or her perspectives and insights.

- **Your Manager.** Find time to meet with your manager to share your personal leadership story. Determine whether your insights are aligned. It helps to have a strong relationship with your manager.

- **Your Team.** Meet with your direct reports and share your personal leadership story with them. See how it affects them. You may find that they have a greater sense of connection to you as a leader. In fact, when we deliver The Leadership Contract™ for Teams program, this activity is really valuable. When peers can share their own stories, it does a lot to strengthen the team.

- **A Leadership Coach.** If you are working with a leadership coach, use one of your coaching sessions to review your personal leadership story with the coach and determine what this means for how you now need to step up as a leader.

- **Your Family.**   Share your personal leadership story with your significant other or even your children. Often, we separate our work lives from our personal lives. Our families have little to no insight into what happens when we are at work. This will help them appreciate you more and possibly understand you better as a person.

 Activity 5.4: Three Ways You Will Share Your Personal Leadership Story

🕐 **15 minutes to complete**

In the space provided, list and describe the three ways you plan to share your leadership story.

_____

_____

_____

_____

_____

Other Ways to Leverage Your Personal Leadership Story

Leaders I've worked with soon come to realize that there are many ways to further leverage their personal leadership stories. Here are some ideas for you to consider and which you may find valuable:

1. Preparing for Job Interviews. Leadership has become a critical priority in almost all organizations. As a result, they want to understand the leadership capabilities of potential employees. If you are in a job search process to secure a new leadership role, you will most likely be asked questions about your leadership. I find that having the leadership story and timeline completed is a great first step in being able to answer these questions effectively. To prepare, review your timeline and pick the one to three stories that best demonstrates your value as an accountable leader. Don't be afraid to share a negative story, but make sure you communicate how you handled it or what you learned from it. What positive outcome came from that negative experience? The more you are able to communicate these leadership stories with conviction, the stronger you will be in the interview.

2. On-Boarding into a New Role. If you do secure a new leadership role, sharing your leadership story with your direct manager and new team is also a good idea. It's a great way for them to know who you are as a leader. It's an opportunity for you to set the tone of being transparent. It also allows you to communicate your leadership expectations of those you lead.

3. Career Discussions. The insights you gain from completing your leadership story provide the foundation for you to have effective career discussions and, in turn, make good career decisions for yourself. You'll have a deep understanding of who you are as a leader, the environment you need to be at your best, and the type of role that you can excel in.

4. Dealing with Challenging Leadership Experiences. Whenever you find yourself going through a difficult period as a leader, it may help to go back to your leadership timeline. Review the other times in your career when you faced obstacles or experienced great difficulty. How did you work your way through those moments? Reconnect with the things you did to help you succeed in the past, and see how you can apply those same strategies in your current situation.

Final Thoughts

The first term of the Leadership Contract states that leadership is a decision and you have to make it. The foundational activity for this term is to be clear on your personal leadership story. Once you do, you will feel you are leading more deliberately and with greater intent. That's the power that comes from knowing who you essentially are as a leader and where you have come from. In the next chapter, you will explore where you are going as a leader and the value you must bring to step up to your core obligations.

Chapter 6

Leadership Is an Obligation—Step Up

For the past few years, *Fortune* magazine has published an annual list of "The World's 50 Greatest Leaders." It recognizes individuals from a cross-section of business, government, philanthropy, sports, and the arts—leaders *Fortune* believes are transforming the world and inspiring others to do the same. It's quite the list of truly accomplished individuals. Here's a sample:

- Businesspeople such as Jeff Bezos from Amazon, Elon Musk from Tesla and SpaceX, and Lisa Su from AMD
- Pope Francis
- Athletes such as LeBron James
- Artists such as Shakira and John Legend
- Political leaders such as German Chancellor Angela Merkel, Taiwan's President Tsai Ing-Wen, and Canada's Prime Minister Justin Trudeau

These and the many others on the list are extraordinary individuals. It is interesting that they make the list not simply because they excel at what they do, but also because they have gone above and beyond in their own leadership roles and have had a significant impact on the world.

Part of the magazine's motivation to create this list is to focus the attention on great leaders because the stories in the media tend to overemphasize the tarnished ones—those leaders embroiled in scandal, corruption, or quite simply ineffective in their roles. *Fortune* also postulates that—in our world of radical transparency and change—truly exceptional, "knockout leadership" is harder to maintain.

Leaders on the list are featured in a brief article that describes who they are and what they've done. As you read each of the stories, you can't help but be inspired. You see, these leaders all seem to rise above their leadership roles and are driven by a broader sense of purpose and obligation. I'd encourage you to review the list every year *Fortune* publishes it.

I'd like you to stop for a moment and think about the following scenario: What if one day in the future you made it to this list? That's right: you!

Fortune has named you as one of the world's greatest leaders. Congratulations! It's quite an accomplishment.

So now the question is: Why did *you* make it onto the list? This is the next foundational activity you will explore. Think of it as a visioning exercise that will better help you understand your core obligation as a leader. This chapter will be all about the second term of the Leadership Contract: Leadership Is an Obligation—Step Up (Figure 6.1).

You will think about how you will create enduring value for your customers, organization, employees, communities, and yourself. Are you ready? Let's get started.

Figure 6.1 Leadership Is an Obligation—Step Up

Activity 6.1: Defining Your Leadership Obligations

45 to 60 minutes to complete all activities in this section

Find a quiet place where you will not be disturbed. Take out the leadership timeline that you completed in the last chapter and review it for inspiration. Now find a pen or pencil. Take a deep breath. Close your eyes and think about a point in the future (five years from now) where you have learned that *Fortune* selected you as one of "The World's 50 Greatest Leaders." Imagine having the magazine in your hands and/or displayed on your tablet. Scroll through the article. See yourself and other leaders showcased in the many articles.

How does this make you feel? Capture your reactions to being featured in this special issue of the magazine.

_____

_____

_____

_____

_____

Let's continue. Now I would like to direct your attention to the following questions. As you begin to complete them, you may find things arise that will get in your way. First, your inner critic jumps in, asking: "Who do you think you are? You don't deserve to see yourself in this way." Ignore your inner critic. This is a visioning exercise. No one else needs to see this work for the time being; it's just for you, so don't be afraid to think big.

Second, you may feel this is a highly egotistical activity. This is what my team and I observe when we do a similar activity in our workshops and seminars. I find many leaders struggle because they feel they are being conceited when they think about their answers to these questions. Unfortunately, this will also limit the quality of your thinking and the ultimate benefit you will receive from this activity. While the focus is on you, you will find the questions are really about how your leadership has made things better for others.

1. What enduring value did you create as an accountable leader, and why did you capture the attention of *Fortune* magazine?

_____

_____

_____

_____

_____

_____

2. In what specific ways did you leave your organization in better shape than you found it?

_____

_____

_____

_____

_____

_____

3. What did your employees say about the impact you had on them as a leader?

_____

_____

_____

_____

_____

_____

4. What did your manager say about the impact you had as a leader?

_____

_____

_____

_____

_____

_____

5. What did your organization's customers say about the value you created for them?

_____

_____

_____

_____

_____

6. What did your colleagues and peers say about the impact and value you had as a leader?

_____

_____

_____

_____

_____

7. What did your important internal and external stakeholders say about the impact you had as a leader?

_____

_____

_____

_____

_____

_____

8. In what ways did your leadership make your community and the world a better place?

_____

_____

_____

_____

_____

_____

9. The article concludes with one statement that captures your primary leadership obligation. What is that statement?

_____

_____

_____

_____

_____

_____

 Reflections

How was that activity for you? If you are like the vast majority of leaders my team and I have worked with, the answer is that it was challenging. In fact, this is one of the most difficult activities we ever do with leaders in our development programs. I believe the biggest reason for its difficulty is that most leaders never engage in this kind of personal visioning. What I've learned is that the more you do it, the easier it becomes, and the better the quality of work you produce and the influence you have with others.

I always am interested in the immediate impact that a clear leadership obligation statement has on a leader. During our development programs, the facilitators go around the room to hear the participants' obligation statements. They are asked to stand and share their statements. What emerges is inspiring.

The participants talk about their visions for creating truly high-performing teams, leaving a lasting legacy in their companies, or the significant impact they will have on their customers and stakeholders.

We never hear obligation statements that are only about personal gains and accomplishments. Every single time, a participant's leadership obligation statement is about the enduring value he or she creates for others: employees, customers, the company, and the community.

And that's the whole point of the second term of the Leadership Contract. Once you are clear about your obligation as a leader, it not only inspires you, but it also inspires those you lead, largely because it's not about you; it's about them.

What also becomes clear is that there is power in sharing your leadership obligation statement with those you lead. It helps them understand what is important to you, what drives you as a leader, and why you make the decisions you do. So take a few minutes to respond to the following question.

 Activity 6.2: Sharing Your Leadership Obligation Statement

 10 minutes to complete

In what ways will you share your leadership obligation statement with others?

_____

_____

_____

_____

_____

What Is Your Desired Value and Impact as a Leader?

The first foundational activity in this chapter was a visioning exercise to help you get clear on what you believe is your primary obligation as a leader. I'd like you to translate the bold and inspiring vision you have for yourself into something that guides your leadership every day in a more practical manner.

To fulfill your leadership obligation, you must be clear on the value you must deliver as a leader as well—the desired impact you will have. The good news is that because of the leadership timeline activity, The Leadership Contract Self-Assessment, and the activity you just completed, you have everything you need to go to the next stage.

 Activity 6.3: Define Your Value and Desired Impact as a Leader

 15 to 30 minutes to conduct planning for activity, plus additional time for interviews and to summarize themes

Before you start this activity, read the section "Define Your Value and Desired Impact as a Leader" in *The Leadership Contract* book.

Define the People to Interview. Think about a number of different people with whom you work; they can be peers, colleagues, customers, key stakeholders, your manager, or some of your direct reports. You will reach out to them and ask them for a fifteen- to twenty-minute meeting during which you will ask a few questions to determine your value and the impact you currently are making as a leader. Through this process, you will learn whether their answers align with your personal vision or understanding of the value and impact you desire to have. While the first activity in this chapter was a visioning exercise, this is in many ways an alignment exercise.

Take a few minutes now to identify six to eight people you want to interview (you can choose more if you wish). Write their names here.

_____

_____

_____

_____

_____

_____

_____

_____

Conduct the Interviews. In your conversations (either face-to-face meetings or phone calls), begin by discussing the work you have been doing in this field guide. Then mention that you want to get their feedback on your leadership and the value you are creating or must create in the future. To help ensure that you have a meaningful conversation, provide the following six questions in advance so your stakeholders can prepare ahead of time.

1. What primary value do I provide as a leader?

2. What impact does my value have on you? On the community of leaders? On the organization?

3. What are my unique strengths as a leader?

4. Where do I need to be more accountable as a leader to have an even greater impact?

5. What blind spots may be getting in my way?

6. What is one consistent action that I must take to have even greater value as a leader and live up to my core obligation?

What is particularly valuable about a process like this is that the feedback you receive is typically candid, direct, and extremely insightful. Instead of guessing what your key stakeholders value, find out directly. The mere act of asking already demonstrates that you are an accountable leader who is committed to living up to your core leadership obligations.

Capture Everyone's Responses Capture all responses using the following tables.

Question	Person 1	Person 2
1. What primary value do I provide as a leader?		
2. What impact does my value have on you?		
3. What are my unique strengths as a leader?		
4. Where do I need to be stronger as a leader to have an even greater impact?		
5. What blind spots may be getting in my way?		
6. What is one consistent action that I must take to provide even greater value as a leader and live up to my core obligation?		

The Leadership Contract Field Guide

Question	Person 3	Person 4
1. What primary value do I provide as a leader?		
2. What impact does my value have on you?		
3. What are my unique strengths as a leader?		
4. Where do I need to be stronger as a leader to have an even greater impact?		
5. What blind spots may be getting in my way?		
6. What is one consistent action that I must take to provide even greater value as a leader and live up to my core obligation?		

Question	Person 5	Person 6
1. What primary value do I provide as a leader?		
2. What impact does my value have on you?		
3. What are my unique strengths as a leader?		
4. Where do I need to be stronger as a leader to have an even greater impact?		
5. What blind spots may be getting in my way?		
6. What is one consistent action that I must take to provide even greater value as a leader and live up to my core obligation?		

The Leadership Contract Field Guide

Question	Person 7	Person 8
1. What primary value do I provide as a leader?		
2. What impact does my value have on you?		
3. What are my unique strengths as a leader?		
4. Where do I need to be stronger as a leader to have an even greater impact?		
5. What blind spots may be getting in my way?		
6. What is one consistent action that I must take to provide even greater value as a leader and live up to my core obligation?		

Summarize Key Themes. Now review all the responses and identify the top three themes for each question. Use the following table to capture your themes and insights.

Question	Top Three Themes/Insights Per Question
1. What primary value do I provide as a leader?	
2. What impact does my value have on you?	
3. What are my unique strengths as a leader?	
4. Where do I need to be stronger as a leader to have an even greater impact?	
5. What blind spots may be getting in my way?	
6. What is one consistent action that I must take to provide even greater value as a leader and live up to my core obligation?	

What insights did you gain about the enduring value you must create?

_____

_____

_____

_____

_____

_____

Revisit the leadership obligation statement you created in the first activity of this chapter. Based on the interviews you conducted, how would you modify this statement? Use this space to capture any changes.

_____

_____

_____

_____

_____

_____

Reflections

What is the value of having a clear obligation statement? This is a question I'm often asked when I deliver presentations.

I have found that the truly accountable and great leaders I've worked with always have a leadership obligation statement that is very clear in their minds. It becomes a central point of focus for their leadership.

Some of you may also be thinking that the activities I asked you to do in this chapter seem like a lot of work. In some ways they are, but chances are you haven't done this type of work before. The personal clarity you gain will help you become a more focused leader. It'll also help you be a more compelling leader because the people around you will see you are driven by an inspiring sense of purpose and obligation.

Just as it's important to create and communicate your personal leadership story, it's also important to create and communicate a clear statement of your leadership obligation. Your personal leadership story communicates who you are as a leader, what has influenced you in the past, and how those experiences have shaped who you are today and who you will be in the future. Your leadership obligation communicates your aspiration for the kind of leader you desire to be, the impact you wish to have, and the enduring value you want to create for your employees, colleagues, customers, stakeholders, and organization. This is what truly accountable leaders do.

Wouldn't you want to work with a leader who has this level of personal clarity and commitment?

 Other Ways to Leverage Your Personal Obligation Statement

There are additional ways to leverage your leadership obligation statement and the work you have done in this chapter. Following are some ideas for you to consider and which you may find valuable:

1. During Job Interviews. In Chapter 5, I explained that sharing your personal leadership story can be an advantage during job interviews. The same is true when

The Leadership Contract Field Guide

you share how you envision your obligations as a leader. The more concrete and specific you are in articulating the value that you will bring as a leader, the more you will set yourself apart from other candidates.

2. Taking on a New Leadership Role.   One of the first important tasks for you to do when you take on a new leadership role is to gain clarity around the leadership obligation you must live up to. The activities in this chapter can help you interview key stakeholders to understand the value you must provide as a leader and the expectations they have of you. Use this information to begin articulating a compelling leadership obligation for yourself. As your role evolves and you spend more time in it, you may find that your leadership obligation also evolves. You will become clear on what matters most. So come back to it from time to time and update it if required. It is also important for you to understand what may undermine your value and what might get in the way of your success.

3. Dealing with Challenging Leadership Experiences.   Whenever you find yourself going through a difficult period as a leader, a compelling leadership obligation can help you reframe your situation and refocus your energy. It's a powerful way to help you rise to the challenges you may face and to find a way forward to lead yourself and your team.

Final Thoughts

This chapter has helped you think about the kind of leader you desire to be. Through the several activities, you now have a clearer sense of the value you must create for your organization, customers, employees, stakeholders, and the communities in which you do business. I encourage you to keep coming back to the ideas in this chapter and the work you have done. Your leadership role continually evolves, and so do your obligations.

Chapter 7

Leadership Is Hard Work—Get Tough

Courage. It's a word that has been coming up a lot in my discussions with leaders. Many are realizing how critical it is to their success. This is not a new idea. In fact, Greek philosopher Aristotle said over 2,000 years ago that *"Courage is the first of human qualities, because it is the quality that guarantees the others."* This is true in life, and it's certainly true in leadership.

Unfortunately, too many leaders lack courage. Many have a tendency to play it safe, take the easy way out, defer unpopular decisions for as long as possible, or stay under the radar at all costs.

As you know, this is what the third term of the Leadership Contract is all about. This term acknowledges the fact that leaders must be courageous because it's not an easy job to be a truly accountable leader. You'll encounter many situations as a leader that require courage and personal toughness to tackle the hard work.

After all, holding people accountable isn't easy. Managing poor performers isn't easy. Accepting candid feedback about how you need to grow as a leader isn't easy. Confronting your personal gaps takes courage.

Instead of getting tough, too many leaders choose to wimp out. But if you are really going to be accountable as a leader, you have to understand that you can't take the easy way out. It's no longer good enough for you to be a bystander. You have to get tough. Everyone—your team, your department, your boss, and your organization—is counting on you to be truly accountable. This will also mean you need to be tough with yourself by building your resolve and personal resilience.

This is going to be the focus of this chapter. We will revisit some of the key ideas of the third term of the Leadership Contract: *Leadership Is Hard Work—Get Tough*.

Figure 7.1 Leadership Is Hard Work—Get Tough

As you complete the activities in this chapter, it is critical that you be prepared to be completely honest with yourself. It's important to not be defensive. This isn't about being the perfect leader; it's about knowing who you are (leadership story), what you are trying to do (obligation), and making sure you don't get into bad habits or let the stress and demands of the role undermine your success.

Since this is the term that leaders often struggle with the most, you will find many activities and reflection exercises in this chapter. Do as many as you feel are necessary to be more accountable in tackling the hard work. I can tell you that working through this chapter will be hard work. So get serious, get focused, and get ready to tackle some hard work!

Are you ready? Let's go!

Activity 7.1: What Hard Work Do You Avoid?

30 to 45 minutes to complete all activities in this section

In *The Leadership Contract,* I shared what I called the hard rule of leadership (Figure 7.2). This rule simply states:

> *If you avoid the hard work of leadership, you'll become a weak leader. If you tackle the hard work of leadership, you'll become a strong leader.*

While you have already done some thinking about this hard rule earlier in this field guide, I'd like to dig a little deeper.

Review the list that follows and check off all items that you know you have a tendency to avoid. You will also have space to add any additional items not covered on my list.

Avoid the hard work **and you become WEAK**

Tackle the hard work **and you become STRONG**

Figure 7.2 The Hard Rule of Leadership

The Hard Work of Leadership I Typically Avoid

☐ Giving direct and candid feedback to my direct reports

☐ Managing a poor performer on my team

☐ Terminating an employee who needs to leave the organization

☐ Calling out the inappropriate behavior of a team member

☐ Having a discussion with a good team member who unfortunately is no longer keeping up

☐ Giving direct feedback to a peer and colleague

☐ Raising a difficult or uncomfortable issue with my manager

☐ Giving personal feedback to any manager about an issue with his or her own leadership

☐ Speaking up when I have a concern about a business decision

☐ Making an important business decision that may be unpopular with my team

☐ Directly addressing conflict between two parties (two employees not getting along or two departments not working well together)

☐ Raising an important issue or concern with senior management

☐ Addressing things at work because I no longer feel committed or engaged in my role

☐ Admitting or recognizing when I have started to settle as a leader

☐ Giving the performance rating an employee deserves rather than just inflating the rating to make my life easier

☐ Taking a stand and having a deep conviction on an important issue

☐ Other: _____

☐ Other: _____

☐ Other: _____

Review all the items you checked off and pick the top two that represent a chronic problem for you. By chronic, I mean things that you find yourself avoiding on a regular and repeated basis. Now for each of those top two, identify what is going on and why you avoid this hard work. Use the space provided to capture your insights.

Challenge One

Describe your first challenge.

_____

_____

Why do you avoid this challenge?

_____

_____

_____

_____

_____

What is preventing you from tackling this head on?

_____

_____

_____

_____

_____

_____

What price are you and your organization paying because you are avoiding it?

_____

_____

_____

_____

_____

If you were truly accountable, what would you do differently?

_____

_____

_____

_____

_____

_____

_____

Challenge Two

Describe your second challenge.

_____

_____

Why do you avoid this challenge?

_____

_____

_____

_____

What is preventing you from tackling this head on?

_____

_____

_____

_____

_____

_____

What price are you and your organization paying because you are avoiding it?

_____

_____

_____

_____

_____

If you were truly accountable, what would you do differently?

_____

_____

_____

_____

_____

_____

_____

Make a personal commitment to improve in these areas. You need courage, and you need to be tough with yourself. Through my own personal leadership role and in working with many leaders, I've found that once you start to build momentum, you start taking on more of the hard work. You'll see yourself growing better and stronger. This will inspire you to do even more.

I have also learned that if you are able to get stronger in the way you tackle the hard work, you will see a huge difference in your leadership. This term of the Leadership Contract will define you as a leader. It will communicate your character. Leadership requires courage and you'll need it to tackle the hard work.

 Activity 7.2: How You May Make the Hard Work Harder

 30 minutes to complete this activity

The previous activity provided you with an initial opportunity to better understand the work you may have a tendency to avoid as a leader. I hope you now better appreciate the price that you, your team, or your organization may be paying as a result.

Now we're going to explore how you might actually get in your own way. We all develop bad habits or patterns of behavior that prevent us from taking on the hard work.

In *The Leadership Contract*, I shared the ten ways leaders make the hard work harder (Figure 7.3).

Go back and read that section again and, as you do, identify the top three ways you make the hard work harder for yourself.

Figure 7.3 The Ten Ways Leaders Make the Hard Work Harder

Write down the top three ways you make the hard work harder for yourself.

_____

_____

_____

As you think of all three, identify how they are undermining the way you lead and eroding your leadership accountability.

_____

_____

_____

_____

As leaders, we all need to develop the ability to enhance our self-awareness of when we make the hard work harder for ourselves. As I said, being a leader isn't easy. The pressures can be intense, and at times we can all fall into one of these traps. By building greater awareness of when it is happening to you, you are better positioned to be more deliberate as a leader. You won't be a victim; you'll be in control.

You may find it valuable to come back to the ten ways leaders make the hard work harder. They are common challenges that we all face as leaders. Many times, we don't just struggle with one of them; we struggle with a few at the same time. For example, if being insecure is a way you make the hard work harder for yourself, then chances are you will also wait for permission.

To ensure your success in tackling the hard work, you'll need to build your resilience and personal resolve. This is where we'll turn to next.

Figure 7.4 Get Tough

Build Resilience and Personal Resolve

The activities we've completed so far in this chapter were designed to build awareness of the hard work you might be avoiding and the ways you might get in your own way as a leader. Now we'll shift focus and explore how to get tough and proactively build the resilience and personal resolve you need to ensure you have the personal capacity to tackle the hard work of a leader (see Figure 7.4).

 Activity 7.3: The Get Tough Self-Assessment

 20 to 30 minutes to complete all the activities in this section

Let's start with a baseline measure of your own resilience and resolve. Think about your current role as a leader and respond to the following questions.

The questions in this self-assessment survey will help you measure your current resilience and resolve. Rate yourself on each question using a 5-point scale, with "1" representing Strongly Disagree (or not at all like me) and "5" representing Strongly Agree (or very much like me).

	Not at All Like Me		Somewhat Like Me		Very Much Like Me
1. Shift How You View the Hard Work					
a. I always see the hard work of leadership as an opportunity to grow and test myself.	①	②	③	④	⑤
b. I am realistic about what I can and can't control.	①	②	③	④	⑤
c. I build self-awareness and I am open to feedback.	①	②	③	④	⑤
d. I am able to monitor when I am making the hard work harder on myself.	①	②	③	④	⑤
2. Develop a Mindset of Resilience					
e. I remain optimistic in the face of adversity.	①	②	③	④	⑤
f. I tend to have a thick skin, which helps me deal with scrutiny and criticism.	①	②	③	④	⑤
g. I manage my emotions and reactions to stressful events in a mature manner.	①	②	③	④	⑤
h. I am able to get myself back on my feet after a setback or disappointment.	①	②	③	④	⑤
3. Build a Strong Sense of Personal Resolve					
i. I have a compelling leadership obligation that helps drive my personal tenacity.	①	②	③	④	⑤
j. I often recall past experiences when I successfully demonstrated resolve.	①	②	③	④	⑤
k. I always manage my personal energy to maintain optimal performance.	①	②	③	④	⑤
l. I regularly draw on my community of leaders for support and encouragement.	①	②	③	④	⑤

Once you have rated yourself, total your scores and enter them here:

Shift How You View the Hard Work	
Develop a Mindset of Resilience	
Build a Strong Sense of Personal Resolve	
Total Score	

Your total responses to your self-assessment will provide a snapshot of your resilience and resolve:

Score	Interpretation
48 to 60	You demonstrate the characteristics needed for strong resilience and resolve. Assess yourself on a regular basis to ensure you maintain this high level and are able to sustain your energy in challenging times.
36 to 47	You have the foundation to demonstrate resilience and resolve. However, there is room for you to get stronger. Make sure you review the ongoing practices to improve as a leader.
35 or below	Your ability to lead in a truly accountable manner is certainly being eroded. You need to understand whether this is a temporary situation or if it's something more permanent. If it is the latter, then you need to take action or risk burnout.

Once you have tallied your scores, answer the following questions:

What personal insights did I gain from completing the Get Tough Self-Assessment?

_____

_____

_____

_____

_____

_____

_____

_____

_____

What specific strengths do I see in myself?

_____

_____

_____

_____

_____

_____

_____

_____

_____

_____

_____

_____

What areas must I improve to increase my resilience and resolve?

_____

_____

_____

_____

_____

_____

_____

_____

_____

_____

Activity 7.4: How to Build Your Resilience and Personal Resolve

45 to 60 minutes to complete all the activities in this section

In Chapter 7 of *The Leadership Contract*, I provide several strategies to help you build your resilience and develop personal resolve. Reread that section of the book. Here I present some additional ideas for you to consider. At the end of this section, I will ask you to identify the practices that will be most meaningful for you in building your resilience and personal resolve.

Essentially, strengthening your resilience and resolve happens in two ways. First, there are a series of ongoing practices you can put in place that ensure you have the reserve power you need to lead. Second, you need a way to handle challenging, stressful, and even overwhelming experiences in the moment.

Ongoing Practices to Build Resilience and Resolve

Let's first look at some ongoing practices for you to consider.

Review Your Personal Leadership Story.   Take out your leadership timeline that you completed earlier. Review those past leadership experiences when you have successfully demonstrated resolve. Uncover what led to your success in the past and think about how you can apply the same lessons in your current situation.

Gain Inspiration from Your Leadership Obligation.   Go back to the previous chapter in this book. Review your leadership obligation statement. Use it to inspire yourself, and let it act as a beacon of light during challenging times. Review it on a regular basis so that it really grounds you as a leader by reminding you of the leader you desire to be. A compelling leadership obligation can pull you forward when you are struggling.

Manage Your Personal Energy.   This includes all the stuff you already know about how to maintain optimal performance—things like regular exercise, eating well, sleep, relaxation or meditation, mindfulness practices, and having a sense of balance in your life.

Draw on Your Community for Support. When the hard work gets the best of you, you might find yourself isolated and cut off from others. Build trusting relationships with colleagues and peers you can rely on for support and encouragement. There is nothing that undermines your resolve more than feeling isolated and disconnected from others. In the following space, identify two to three colleagues whom you trust and can go to when you need support.

_____

_____

_____

In-the-Moment Practices to Maintain Your Resilience and Resolve

A series of in-the-moment practices can also help you maintain your resilience and resolve. These practices are valuable because every day you may encounter events that surprise you. Many leaders can become consumed by such events. Thinking about them completely takes up your mental and emotional energy. Suddenly, you realize you've essentially wasted a day.

Accountable leaders respond differently and reframe the situation, mitigating the negative impact so they can keep working at an optimal level. The key is to have what I call a good "reset" button—one that enables you to reframe, refocus, and move on in any given situation.

So the next time something happens during your day that tests your resolve, observe how you respond. Do you let the event disrupt your entire day? Or do you take it for what it is, learn from it, and move on to the next thing?

It's helpful in these moments to do what I call a mental and emotional reset. Four actions will help you gain a better handle in the moment when you are challenged and under stress.

Calm Yourself. Take a deep breath and get in touch with your reactions to the situation. Don't act immediately. One powerful strategy is to learn how to leverage the power of rhythmic breathing. Dr. Marlynn Wei, a board-certified Harvard and Yale-trained psychiatrist and yoga instructor, shares her insights in her book (co-authored with Dr. James Grove) *The Harvard Medical School Guide to Yoga*. Her strategy is based on the following steps that you can follow when you need to do a reset during your day. Use your smartphone to set a timer for two or three minutes.

1. Close your eyes and focus on your breath.
2. Take a deep breath through your nose while you count to five.
3. Hold your breath for five counts.
4. Exhale for five counts.
5. Repeat for the remaining time.

It's easy to remember. Five steps. Five counts where you breathe in. Five counts where you hold your breath. Five counts to exhale. Repeat.

Practice these steps right now! Grab your smartphone or a timer. Set it for three minutes and follow the five steps above.

Wei also states that while this strategy is invaluable in challenging moments, it's also good to practice it on a regular basis throughout your day. The approach is quick and simple, but it has an important impact on calming you down and changing your state so you are able to see things from a new perspective.

Challenge yourself to pause and do a couple of minutes of rhythmic breathing before a meeting or a conference call, an important presentation, or a challenge conversation. You may find it valuable to also practice at home. Take a few minutes to pause and breathe before you enter your home after work, or before a difficult conversation with a family member.

The more you can embed this practice in simple things you face each day, the more it will become automatic.

Reframe the Situation.   With a calm mind, come back to the situation. What's the hidden opportunity that has emerged? In what ways can you creatively turn the situation around? How can you see your situation with fresh eyes?

Learn from the Moment. Ask yourself what you can learn from the situation. How might you approach it differently next time? Remember that every moment is a new leadership experience, one that may appear on your leadership timeline at a future date.

Inspire Yourself. Based on what you have learned, leverage the energy to propel yourself forward. Use the lessons as inspiration. See the moment as a challenge—a test to see how good you really are as a leader.

As you review the strategies explained above and in Chapter 7 of *The Leadership Contract*, identify three specific strategies that you will implement in your leadership role.

_____

_____

_____

_____

_____

Learn How to Have Tough Conversations

One resounding theme that has emerged in my work on leadership accountability over the past five years is that *we need leaders who have the courage to have a whole host of tough conversations*. One thing I've become absolutely clear on is how much our organizations suffer because tough conversations are avoided.

As the hard rule of leadership states, when you avoid the hard work, you become weak. When you avoid having a tough conversation you become weak, as does your colleague—and even your company. Not avoiding tough conversations is a significant developmental topic for the majority of leaders with whom I've worked. Leaders avoid a number of tough conversations. Here's a common list I've gathered in talking to leaders like you:

- You have to talk to a direct report about poor performance.

- You have a direct report who was once really effective in his role, but now is struggling and no longer keeping up.

- You need to tell someone you don't see her career progressing in the way she desires or believes it's going.

- You need to provide feedback to someone about a behavioral style issue that is getting in his way (for example, talking too much during meetings, being a gossip, or chronic tardiness).

- You need to challenge a peer or colleague for bad leadership behavior.

- You feel compelled to raise an important but controversial issue with your manager or the senior executive team.

 Activity 7.5: The Tough Conversations We Avoid

30 minutes to complete all the activities in this section

Review the list above and write down the kinds of conversations you know you struggle with and typically avoid.

_____

_____

_____

_____

_____

_____

Figure 7.5 How to Have Tough Conversations

I call these "tough" conversations because they are not easy ones to have. They are tough for you as the leader and tough for the person with whom you are having the conversation. You may have a tendency to avoid the tough conversations because it makes you uncomfortable, or you don't want to deal with the reaction the other person may have (for example, getting angry, starting to cry in your presence, or eroding his or her level of engagement).

I have also found that what may hold some leaders back from having tough conversations is that they worry about the technique or how to structure the discussion. This certainly can be a barrier, but I find it can also be an excuse. The *how* is important. You certainly shouldn't have a tough conversation when you are angry or in a vengeful state. Next, I share a process that will help you improve your ability to have tough conversations (see Figure 7.5).

Let's spend some time discussing each of the components required to have tough conversations successfully. The first four components will help you to prepare for a tough conversation. The second four components will help you during the actual tough conversation.

Prepare to Have the Tough Conversation

1. Focus on How Much You Care. In my experience, the first step is actually to focus on how much you care about the person, your company, and your collective success. When you begin from this starting point, having the conversation is easier because, at the end of the day, the person will know you have his back. He may not like what he hears, but he will appreciate your courage and the fact that you're looking out for his best interests. You will actually strengthen the level of trust between the two of you.

2. Practice the Conversation.   It's helpful to practice having the conversation in your own mind, or even practice it with a trusted colleague. During your practice, anticipate how the other the person might react. It's also a good idea to anticipate how you will react. Practice different ways of approaching the conversation until you find the one you are comfortable with.

3. Mention That You Need to Have a Tough Conversation.   Being transparent like this gives the person a heads up that the discussion is not going to be easy for her or for you. I find it also gets people's immediate attention. Be firm and unwavering so the person knows it is an important conversation that you need to have with her.

4. Determine Whether the Person Is Ready to Have the Conversation.   When you give him a heads up, you may immediately find that he reacts or becomes defensive. You need to determine whether he can actually have the tough conversation at that moment, or whether you need to schedule another time. Make sure you remain calm and do not react emotionally yourself.

Have the Tough Conversation

5. Be Direct and Factual.   Sometimes leaders muster up the courage to have a tough conversation and then undermine themselves by being evasive and unclear. This can confuse your colleague. If you need to, prepare your thoughts ahead of time. Don't evade or try to soften the issue; address the core issue frankly with the facts.

6. Show the Impact of the Behavior.   Many times, people do not fully appreciate the impact of their own behavior. It can be a blind spot for them. So it is important to describe the gap between the individual's behavior and the desired outcomes you are both trying to achieve. Clearly state how her behavior may be undermining her success, credibility, or reputation.

7. Encourage an Honest Response. Invite your colleague to respond to your points. Be open to disagreement and debate. Remain calm, especially if the person gets emotional. Sometimes that is what is necessary. For example, if you know the person may start crying, have a box of tissue and a glass of water ready to help him or her through it. If he or she has a tendency to react defensively and with anger, stay calm and try not to react yourself.

8. Reaffirm Your Positive Intention. It's helpful to reassure the individual that your intentions are positive. Acknowledge points of strength to leverage and progress made in addition to constructive feedback. Finally, remind her that you have her back and you are available for additional support.

You will find that once you are comfortable putting this approach in place, the tough conversations will get easier. Over time, the tough conversation will still be tough because you must confront a difficult topic; however, it won't be as tough on you or the people you are working with.

 Activity 7.6: It's Time for You to Have the Tough Conversations

Using the steps above, think of a current tough conversation you need to have. Write down the name of the person with whom you need to have a tough conversation and describe the situation.

Now answer the following questions to help you prepare for the conversation.

1. **Focus first on how much you care.** Think of the person you need to have your tough conversation with. Think about why you care about this person and his or her success. Focus on visceral feelings. Write down why you care about this person's success.

---

2. **Practice the conversation.** Identify a trusted colleague with whom you can practice. Who is that colleague?

_____

_____

_____

3. **Mention that you need to have a tough conversation.** How will you bring this up? Why do you feel it will be tough for that person? For you?

_____

_____

_____

4. **Determine whether the person is ready to have the conversation.** How will you gauge whether the person is ready? Sometimes all you need to do is ask.

_____

_____

_____

5. **Be direct and factual.** What feedback must you share? Write it down. Make sure it is direct (not sugar-coated) and factual (supported by facts).

_____

_____

_____

6. **Explain the impact of the behavior.** Write down how the person's behavior is undermining his or her success.

_____

_____

_____

_____

_____

7. **Encourage an honest response.** How will you encourage an honest response?

_____

_____

_____

8. **Reaffirm your positive intention.** What statements or words can you share that will reaffirm your positive intention in having this conversation? Write them down.

_____

_____

_____

 ## Other Ways to Leverage the Ideas in This Chapter

I'm sure that as you worked through the activities in this chapter you have thought of additional ways to leverage your insights. The most common insight generated by leaders I've worked with is the immediate value they see in leveraging the activities in this chapter with their teams and colleagues. Here are some ideas for you to consider and which you may find valuable:

1. Discuss the Hard Rule of Leadership with Your Team. Understanding how a team tackles or avoids the hard work can be extremely powerful. My team and I find it's often a difficult discussion for the team to have. However, if you can be tough and have the discussion, you will find the team becomes more open and transparent with one another. The key is not to be judgmental, but rather to understand where the team members need to be more deliberate and decisive in tackling their individual and collective hard work. If you want to drive greater leadership accountability with your team, then discuss the hard work the team is avoiding and create a game plan to improve.

2. Explore Team Resilience and Resolve. The ideas of resilience and resolve are also important to teams and can impact performance. Consider completing the Get Tough Self-Assessment as a team. Use the results to identify strengths and gaps. Focus on how the team can build more resilience and resolve to drive better business results.

3. Create the Expectations and Conditions for Tough Conversations. In this chapter, you explored what it takes to effectively have tough conversations. Imagine if your team were able to do the same? Spend time discussing these ideas with your team and create a team culture in which having tough conversations is expected and valued. It will completely change the dynamics on your team. As I'm sure you can appreciate, this will not be easy at first. But if you stay with it, if you keep holding your team accountable, you will reach a point at which the tough conversations will not be so tough after all.

4. Have Tough Conversations with Peers and Colleagues Across the Organization. Having a tough conversation with a direct report or with your team is challenging enough for many leaders. However, the real need in most companies is for leaders to have tough conversations with their peers from other departments or divisions. There are simply too many important conversations that are not taking place, and it's slowing down progress and impeding organizational performance. To be truly accountable, you must do a better job of having the conversations with your peers and colleagues from other departments. One way is for you to share the ideas and activities in this chapter with them. Help them understand why these tough conversations must happen and the price you are all paying when you avoid them. Work with your colleagues to tackle those complicated, complex, and thorny issues. If you do, you immediately take your company to a higher level of performance. What tough conversation must you have with a peer or colleague right now? Get to it now. Don't waste any more time!

Final Thoughts

It's time we create organizations in which we can have candid, frank, and adult conversations about our business and about each other and our collective performance. Our inability to do so wastes time, creates roadblocks that slow down our progress, and interferes with our success. Here's your challenge: *to be the leader who commits to doing the hard work, maintain your resilience and resolve, and have the tough conversations in your organization.*

Chapter 8

Leadership Is a Community—Connect

L et's start this chapter with a quick activity. I'd like you to close your eyes for a moment and think about the attributes of the leadership culture that would enable you to be at your best as a leader. Imagine a leadership culture so vibrant, so inspirational, and so supportive that it drives you and your colleagues to achieve higher levels of performance each and every day.

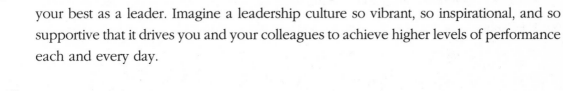

Activity 8.1: Describe the Leadership Culture That Would Enable You to Be at Your Best as a Leader

10 minutes to complete

Find a pen or pencil and write down all the attributes that come to mind in the following space.

_____

_____

_____

_____

_____

I've asked this same question of leaders around the world. It is always surprising to me how consistent the themes are that emerge from our discussions. The attributes of truly compelling leadership cultures most frequently shared are:

- Leaders have a high sense of trust with each other.

- Mutual support is very strong.

- They have strategic clarity.

- Leaders are committed and passionate about the company.

- There is positive energy in the company.

- Leaders respect and value the capabilities of everyone.

- They hold each other accountable.

- They give each other feedback to ensure they are successful.

- Politics and grandstanding are absent.

- Leaders feel they can ask for help when they need it.

How similar is this list to the one you just created? I suspect there will be some similarities and overlap. This is actually one of the most surprising things I've discovered in my travels—mainly, how consistent the responses are to this question. It seems we all know how to describe the attributes of a leadership culture in which we'll be at our best.

Yet what truly puzzles me is that, despite this, why do so few of us work in these types of leadership cultures? And why are they so hard to create and sustain?

In my experience, I find few of us work and lead in organizations with strong leadership cultures. Instead, we find ourselves in cultures where we are continually working at cross-purposes with colleagues. Getting anything meaningful done feels next to impossible some days. We experience low levels of trust and support. Engagement among employees and leaders is low. Internal politics consume people. It's no wonder my global research has found that only 27 percent of organizations surveyed believe they have a strong leadership culture.

To me, this issue is of paramount importance. We need to figure out as leaders how to build strong leadership cultures. The way leaders work today is changing before our very eyes. When I started working early in my career, organizations were all about hierarchy, silos, centralized decision making, and the hoarding of power and information.

Today, leadership is more distributed and networked than ever before. We work in teams that are expected to collaborate and innovate. Those old structures based on hierarchy and silos must give way to more horizontal and integrated ways of working. To be successful, we must redefine how we work and lead.

Most of us are ready for this change. We yearn for an experience of work that is more fulfilling, gratifying, and rewarding than it is today.

I believe this is why the fourth term of the Leadership Contract—*Leadership Is a Community—Connect*—has resonated so much with leaders and companies (Figure 8.1).

We are all beginning to recognize that we need to evolve how we lead and to do it in the spirit of community, rather than holding on to old and outdated models and structures.

This is not work for the faint of heart. Changing the culture of an organization is some of the most challenging work there is for leaders. But as a leader, this is the work you're being called to do, so the rest of this chapter will help you achieve success.

Figure 8.1 Leadership Is a Community—Connect

Leadership Is a Community—Connect

We will begin by assessing the kind of leadership culture you currently have in your organization. Then, we will look at what a strong community of leaders actually looks like. Finally, we will discuss how you can create it within your organization, team, or department.

Your Experience with Leadership Cultures

In *The Leadership Contract,* I described three types of leadership cultures that I typically see in organizations. Go to that section in Chapter 8 of the book, read the descriptions of each of those cultures, and then answer the following questions. As you do, make sure you capture what it felt like working in that environment. Also identify whether the culture motivated you to bring your best every day.

 Activity 8.2: Your Experience with Different Leadership Cultures

30 minutes to complete all activities in this section

What was your experience working in a Rotting of Zombies culture?

_____

_____

_____

_____

_____

_____

What was your experience working in a League of Heroes culture?

_____

_____

_____

_____

_____

What was your experience working in a Stable of Thoroughbreds culture?

_____

_____

_____

_____

_____

When I discuss these types of leadership cultures with leaders, everyone has had direct experience with one or all three of them at some point in his or her career. People can describe with disgust the feelings of apathy that consume a zombie organization. They feel resentful about how so much energy and potential from employees is squandered and wasted.

Many talk about what happens in a hero culture—the centralized decision making and autocratic way the company is run. These things can take a toll on people in different ways. This type of culture doesn't create opportunities for people to lead because only one leader is allowed to exist.

The conversations continue to be interesting when leaders talk about the hyper-competitive climate of a thoroughbred culture, often described as a cutthroat or dog-eat-dog culture. Over time, this wears people down. As one leader said in a session, "It is a soul-destroying place to be."

How did your own responses align with what I just shared from other leaders?

Assessing the Leadership Culture in Your Organization

The activity above introduced three kinds of dysfunctional leadership cultures and the experiences you may have had with them. In many ways, they were simply metaphors to describe the leadership cultures that can exist in a company.

Let's build on this work and start thinking about your current organization. For this next activity, I'm going to ask you to do a few things you may not be used to doing. Often when thinking about culture, it's helpful to come at the topic from a different way of thinking. So I'm going to ask you to complete a few activities.

The first activity will help you to think about your current leadership culture and create your own metaphor for it. The second will help you to create a drawing or cartoon of your current leadership culture.

Activity 8.3: A Metaphor for Your Organization's Leadership Culture

10 to 15 minutes to complete

Many interesting metaphors emerge when we do this activity with leaders. I've heard of all kinds of metaphors; here are some examples:

- *"Our leadership culture is like the Titanic. We've hit an iceberg and we are sinking fast."*
- *"Our leadership culture is like a traffic jam on a congested freeway. Everyone is honking their horns, yelling at each other and getting nowhere."*
- *"Our leadership culture is like a runaway train. There's no conductor, we're traveling at lightning speed, but no one knows where we are headed."*
- *"Our culture is like a pack of barking dogs. Everyone seems to be growling at each other."*

You get the idea and the power of using a metaphor. They seem to capture the core essence of a leadership culture.

Write down a metaphor that you believe describes the leadership culture in your current organization.

_____

_____

_____

_____

_____

Activity 8.4: Create a Drawing of Your Organization's Leadership Culture

10 to 15 minutes to complete

In 2011, Manu Cornet, an artist, musician, and software engineer at Google, created a set of six images (see Figure 8.2) to capture the cultures of large technology companies such

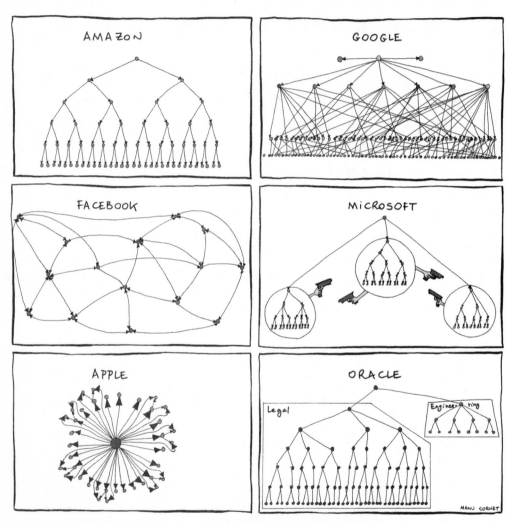

Figure 8.2 Images of Cultures of Technology Companies
Permission granted by Manu Cornet for use of his images and drawings.

as Apple, Google, Microsoft, and others. His satirical diagrams went viral and *The New York Times* even ran a story about them a few years later.

I can understand why Cornet's diagrams captured the imagination of so many people. As you can see, his images are fun and yet give you a clear sense of an organization's leadership culture from Cornet's perspective. Review the images of the six different companies and think about the differences you see.

I find these images interesting because I've used a similar approach in my work with senior leaders when they were attempting to transform their leadership cultures. In these circumstances, I have found it valuable to ask them to create an image, drawing, or cartoon of their organization's current leadership culture. Like the metaphor activity above, drawing an image that depicts your leadership culture seems to tap a different region of your brain and get at the heart of any issue. Then I ask them to define what in the current culture must be kept and what must evolve for the future.

So now it's your turn. I'm going to ask you to create your own image, drawing, or cartoon for your company's current leadership culture. Now I know some of you are already resisting this idea. You may be thinking to yourself, "I can't draw. I'm not artist."

I hear you. I certainly am no artist myself. The good news is that you do not have to be one to complete this activity. Some of the best drawings or cartoons I've seen have been really simple ones that beautifully capture the essence of an idea, just as Cornet has done with his images above.

Simply think about your current leadership culture. Really get into how it makes you feel, and come up with an image that captures it. Give it a try.

Activity 8.5: Draw the Leadership Culture of Your Organization

15 to 20 minutes to complete

In the box below or on a separate sheet of paper, create a drawing or cartoon that you believe best depicts your current leadership culture.

The Community of Leaders Manifesto: Making the Intangible Tangible

The activities above were focused on getting a clearer sense of the current leadership culture in your organization. The metaphors and drawings were an attempt to make something that is often seen as an intangible more tangible.

This is the primary reason why I think so many leaders and organizations struggle with creating and sustaining strong leadership cultures: It just feels too intangible.

Many feel it's amorphous. One CEO I worked with referred to leadership culture as "Jell-O: this wobbly, jiggly thing that I just can't get hold of."

I can understand why some leaders, particularly the hard-nosed business types, see it that way. So to help those leaders better understand culture, I created The Community of Leaders Manifesto, which I shared in *The Leadership Contract*. It was my way of making leadership culture into something much more tangible, and therefore changeable. Here it is again for your reference (Figure 8.3).

This manifesto makes explicit the behaviors and habits we need to avoid as leaders, and the leadership decision we must personally make to bring about a different kind of

WE ARE **DONE WITH THE OLD MODEL** OF LEADERSHIP THAT HAS GLORIFIED HEROES.

WE ARE DONE SETTLING FOR **MEDIOCRITY.** WE WILL NOT BE **LAME LEADERS.** WE WILL STOP GOING THROUGH **THE MOTIONS.** WE WILL PUT AN END TO THE **ISOLATION** THAT WE FEEL EVERY DAY.

WE WILL **NOT BE DISCONNECTED FROM ONE ANOTHER.** WE WILL **NOT PUT UP WITH A CLIMATE OF APATHY** AND LOW TRUST. WE WILL **PUT AN END TO ALL THE INFIGHTING** AND COMPETITION. WE WILL STOP BUILDING SILOS. WE WILL **STOP WORKING AT CROSS-PURPOSES.** INSTEAD,

WE RESOLVE TO **CREATE A STRONG COMMUNITY OF LEADERS**—ONE WHERE THERE IS **HIGH CLARITY** ON WHAT WE ARE TRYING TO ACCOMPLISH AS LEADERS TO **MAKE OUR ORGANIZATION GREAT.**

WE WILL **SHARE A COLLECTIVE ASPIRATION** AND PASSION FOR **GREAT LEADERSHIP.** WE WILL **SET AN EXAMPLE** TO OTHER ORGANIZATIONS.

WE WILL BUILD THE **BEST LEADERS** IN OUR INDUSTRY.

WE WILL OPERATE AS **ONE COMPANY.**

WE WILL BE ALIGNED TO **OUR STRATEGY.**

WE WILL **DRIVE COLLABORATION AND INNOVATION** ACROSS OUR ORGANIZATION. WE WILL **BUILD STRONG RELATIONSHIPS** WITH ONE ANOTHER. WE WILL **MAKE EACH OTHER STRONGER.** ONCE WE BUILD A STRONG COMMUNITY OF LEADERS, IT WILL BECOME OUR **ULTIMATE DIFFERENTIATOR.** IT WILL BE OUR **TRUE AND EVERLASTING SOURCE OF COMPETITIVE ADVANTAGE.** **IT ALL STARTS WITH EACH ONE OF US.** IT ALL STARTS WITH A DECISION TO LEAD MORE DELIBERATELY—WITH GREATER PERSONAL **CLARITY AND COMMITMENT.**

Figure 8.3 The Community of Leaders Manifesto

leadership culture. Go back to it now and, as you read through it, be deliberate in looking for the behaviors you and your fellow leaders must stop perpetuating in your organization. At the same time, I'd like you to identify the behaviors that you must embrace in order to bring about a stronger leadership culture.

Activity 8.6: The Community of Leaders Manifesto

20 to 30 minutes to complete

As you read The Community of Leaders Manifesto, which current behaviors must you and your fellow leaders stop perpetuating in your organization? Write down the top three.

_____

_____

_____

Identify the top three behaviors you and your fellow leaders must embrace in order to bring about a strong leadership culture in your organization. Write down the top three.

_____

_____

_____

As you can see, The Community of Leaders Manifesto outlines the commitment that you must make to create a strong community of leaders in your organization. It clarifies what you and your fellow leaders need to aspire to and the behaviors you must commit to living every day. Use the manifesto as an ongoing source of inspiration for yourself and your fellow leaders.

Share it with the employees you lead. Tell them this is the culture you desire to create within your own team, department, or line of business.

Be a Community Builder Every Day

In the end, building a strong leadership culture means bringing about a new way of working and relating with your peers and colleagues. Relationships are the lifeblood of a strong community. You have an accountability as a leader to become a community builder. Unfortunately, I can tell you with a high degree of confidence that you are most likely not very good at it. Hear me out.

In all my work with leaders, I have found that only a small minority are truly relationship-oriented. How many times do you actually call a colleague to see how he or she is doing? How many times do you get out of your office and take the elevator to another floor to sit and visit with a colleague? I've seen so many instances of leaders (sometimes really senior ones) meeting colleagues for the first time during a meeting I was facilitating. They've worked together in the same company for years, but they never bothered to reach out to one another.

Everyone has the best intentions. But good intentions are not enough when it comes to leadership. It's a lot like what happens in our personal lives. Has this ever happened to you? You're out somewhere with your spouse or significant other. You meet old friends you haven't seen in years. You have a quick chat, and then what do both of you say to one another? "We should get together soon!" You even exchange telephone numbers so you can text each other. You both have the best intentions to set up a time to see one another again, but do you? Most of the time, you don't. Your life gets busy, and weeks and then months go by. No text. No opportunity to reconnect.

The same thing happens in our workplaces. You probably have the best intentions to connect. But you don't. You are buried by all your projects and your workload. You are always making trade-offs: I can't spare the thirty minutes to meet that person; I need it for my team. Or, my manager needs my help on a burning issue.

We need to get better at being community builders and establishing stronger relationships with our peers and colleagues. You cannot build community among strangers. It will never happen.

As I write about in *The Leadership Contract*, the good news is that building a strong community of leaders rests on a few simple actions—five of them, actually—that you can implement every single day. Review that section now.

 Activity 8.7: The Relationships You Need to Make Stronger

 30 to 45 minutes to complete all activities in this section

I'd like you to first think of three relationships that you know you must make stronger with a peer or colleague. Here are some prompts to help you identify the ones you need to focus on. As you read them, write down the names of colleagues where appropriate.

1. **A strained relationship.** You may have a colleague with whom you know the relationship is strained or distant, or conflict has taken over. You know you need to improve the relationship because the current dynamic is getting in the way. Which of your colleagues falls under this category?

_____

_____

2. **A new relationship.** You may have a colleague who just joined your company and with whom you will need to collaborate. Make it a priority to get to know this person. Who falls under this category?

_____

_____

3. **A weak relationship.** You may have a colleague with whom the relationship is weak. It's not necessarily negative; you've just never paid any attention to that person or his or her team. Which colleague would you identify in this category?

_____

_____

4. **An underutilized relationship.** You have a good relationship with a peer or colleague, but you may not really understand what she and her team do. By learning more about what she does, you will find greater synergies and ways to support each other's successes. Who falls under this category for you?

_____

_____

Based on this analysis, what are the top three relationships that you need to improve immediately?

_____

_____

Which of the following strategies can you put in place over time so that you make the relationship stronger, build a sense of community, and drive better business results for your company? Complete the table: Identify the top three colleagues along the top row. Then review the five behaviors to strengthen your relationships and write in the appropriate box what you specifically intend to do.

	Colleague 1	Colleague 2	Colleague 3
Name:			
Connect Informally: Spend time over coffee breaks getting to know colleagues personally.			
Connect Over a Meal: I find there is something important about sharing food with colleagues: It builds stronger connections.			
Connect across Departments: Invite colleagues from different business units to your own meetings to learn about what they do and how you can work more effectively together.			
Connect via Technology: At times, you and your colleagues are in different parts of the world, so you'll need to be good at connecting via technology.			
Connect People to One Another: You may have a colleague with whom the relationship is already strong. But you can make it stronger by connecting that colleague to other people you know.			

It's always remarkable to me how small actions can make a big difference. Stephen Covey wrote in his book, *The Seven Habits of Highly Effective People*, that in relationships *"the small things are the big things."* The small actions you can embrace that will build high-trust relationships with peers and colleagues are just that—small, simple things you can do every day. But over time, these small actions build and create strong bonds with the leaders you work with. These actions aren't complicated. You just must commit and be accountable to valuing and building relationships.

 ## Other Ways to Leverage The Community of Leaders Manifesto

A strong leadership culture is a powerful force in any company. You can leverage this power further by extending the use of The Community of Leaders Manifesto. Here are a few examples that I've picked up in my discussions with leaders:

1. With Your Team.   Leaders have told me that they have used the manifesto with the teams they lead. They devote time at a team meeting to read the document. They then discuss the extent to which the team's culture demonstrates the behaviors of a strong community of leaders. They also do check-ins during their regular meetings to keep the manifesto top of mind and ensure everyone is accountable for bringing the behaviors to life.

2. With Cross-Functional Teams.   These types of teams exist in most organizations. Typically, they are working on a critical initiative for their company. These teams bring together leaders from different departments, representing differing areas of expertise. I've come across several examples of how these teams have used The Community of Leaders Manifesto at the start of their work. It helps them establish a common set of standards for the kind of team they desire to be, and the critical behaviors that will drive their success.

3. To Align Teams After a Merger or Acquisition.   Another client shared how they leveraged The Community of Leaders Manifesto to help new teams after the merger of two companies. Again, like the examples above, the manifesto serves to help teams define the key behaviors leaders must demonstrate to drive success.

4. During a Job Search to Determine the Leadership Culture of a Company. One of the questions I am often asked by leaders when they are searching for a job is: How can I determine the leadership culture of a company that I'm considering joining? This is an important question because you want to make sure that you join a company with a great leadership culture. I would suggest having the courage to ask some direct and even tough questions about the culture. Use The Community of Leaders Manifesto and ask pointed questions about the company's culture to determine whether it is lame and weak or vibrant and strong.

It's important to remember that few companies have strong leadership cultures. If you will recall, our global research showed that only 27 percent of companies we surveyed said they had a strong leadership culture. So while looking for a great leadership culture is important, you may not find many. In this case, do not get discouraged. You want to find a company that knows its leadership culture is not strong, but they have a keen motivation to get stronger. So there may be a great opportunity for you as a new leader to help transform the company's leadership culture. The Community of Leaders Manifesto will help you assess a company, and then bring in an approach to help improve things.

Final Thoughts

If you commit to being a community builder in your organization, you will help create a climate of high trust and support, which are the bedrock of strong leadership cultures. So remember to connect. Don't allow yourself to become so focused on your work that you are always head down and not looking up, reaching out, and building relationships with colleagues. This is going to be the new work of leadership in the future. Be that leader!

The Regular Practices for Living the Leadership Contract

I n *The Leadership Contract,* I also presented a series of what I called "regular practices" to help leaders live the Leadership Contract and, more specifically, translate and transfer the four terms into your leadership role.

THE LEADERSHIP CONTRACT FIELD GUIDE
The Roadmap to Becoming a Truly Accountable Leader

SECTION ONE The Core Ideas	SECTION TWO The Foundational Practices for Living the Leadership Contract	SECTION THREE The Regular Practices for Living the Leadership Contract	SECTION FOUR The Turning Points of Leadership

⑨ Regular Practices for Living the
Leadership Contract
Commit to daily, weekly, quarterly,
and annual practices to sustain
your leadership accountability

Chapter 9: Regular Practices for Living the Leadership Contract
This chapter presents a series of activities that you can complete on a daily, weekly, quarterly, and annual basis. You can review them all and then select the activities that will be most meaningful to you.

Regular Practices for Living the Leadership Contract

S o far in this field guide, you have had the opportunity to learn more about the core ideas of leadership accountability and the four terms of the Leadership Contract. You've completed foundational activities that will provide a solid basis for you to become a truly accountable leader. Many of these activities are part of leadership programs that my colleagues and I deliver to companies with leaders like you. After these sessions, the number one question my team and I hear from our clients is: How do we ensure we sustain all this great work?

It's an important question because, in the end, if leaders cannot translate and transfer their insights back into their leadership roles, then we haven't made the changes we need to make.

This brings us to the purpose of this chapter: to present you with a set of regular practices designed to help you live the four terms of the Leadership Contract every day and to help you become the accountable leader your company needs.

In this chapter, you'll find activities that you can implement on a daily, weekly, quarterly, and annual basis. These activities have been tried and tested by leaders in our client organizations. We know that they work. Feel free to start with the activities that sound most meaningful to you. You can work on all of them, or just the vital few that matter in your role.

Daily Actions for Living the Leadership Contract

As I shared in *The Leadership Contract*, I was inspired by a client who told me how much she connected with the four terms. She then challenged herself to go further than a one-time commitment to living those principles. She converted the four terms into four questions that she said she was going to ask herself at the start of each day. I really liked her questions and decided to include them in the book. Here they are:

1. What leadership decision do I have to make today?
2. What leadership obligation do I have to live up to today?
3. What hard work do I have to tackle today as a leader?
4. Which relationship with a colleague do I need to make stronger today to continue to build a community of leaders?

I find these questions to be both simple and practical. Asking these questions is a great way to translate and transfer the four terms into your role day to day. My team also created a small job aid that summarizes these questions. We share these cards with leaders during keynote presentations, workshops, and seminars. Everyone loves them, and many ask to have additional copies to share with their peers and direct reports. Many leaders have shared how valuable the questions have been to them.

 Activity 9.1: The Daily Experiment

 10 minutes each day to complete

Try this experiment for yourself:

Pick a week at work, and for five consecutive days ask yourself the questions above at the beginning of each day. At the end of each day, take a few minutes to reflect on how you showed up as a leader. Use the template that follows to capture any observations or insights you had as you deliberately focused on living the four terms of the Leadership Contract.

Living the Four Terms of the Leadership Contract: The Four Questions Experiment

	How did asking yourself the four questions help you lead in a more accountable manner?
Day 1	
Day 2	
Day 3	
Day 4	
Day 5	

🔍 **Reflections**

How did the experiment go for you? Leaders we have worked with often mention how these simple questions help them be more deliberate and intentional. They also share how, over time, the questions become automatic, meaning you naturally think about them as you are leading. This is the ideal outcome: When these questions become part of how you naturally think, then you know you are on your way to truly being accountable in your role.

Other leaders have told me that these questions are helpful in specific moments while leading. For example, a leader may be in a really difficult meeting, struggling to know how to handle the situation. Suddenly, the questions come to mind. The leader does a quick in-the-moment gut check, which acts as a mental reset. As a result, the leader knows how to step up in that situation. You may find the same thing will happen to you as you focus on these questions more and more.

Weekly Actions for Living the Four Terms of the Leadership Contract

I've been writing my *Gut Check for Leaders* blog for quite a number of years. I post my blog once a week. The title is framed in the form of a question because I want each post to stimulate critical thinking and reflection on the part of the reader. I also try to keep the blog short and easy to read.

I believe that if we each develop a habit of thinking about our leadership roles, even for a few minutes every week, it will engrain the discipline we need to be more accountable leaders.

I've been truly grateful for the responses from my readers. In fact, many of my clients tell me they have incorporated the blogs as part of their leadership development programs. They share the blogs internally with their leaders. Some actually create a learning assignment around the blogs. One client shared how they structured the learning activity to support each blog. They send out a blog with a worksheet that has the following questions:

1. What are the implications of this blog's topic to my own leadership role?
2. How can the ideas in this blog help me be a more accountable leader?

That's it. Simple and straightforward—but a great way to spark some good reflection about your leadership role each week.

Activity 9.2: The Weekly Gut Check for Leaders

🕐 **15 to 20 minutes per week to complete**

If you believe this weekly activity will be valuable to you, then go to www.theleadershipcontract.com and subscribe to my blog. It will be in your inbox every week. Once you read the blog, remember to ask yourself the two questions on the previous page.

Quarterly Actions for Living the Four Terms of the Leadership Contract

You can put two key quarterly practices in place to help sustain your efforts to live up to the four terms of the Leadership Contract.

- First, we will explore setting up a Leadership Accountability Peer Group with your peers.
- Second, I'll explain how to have an annual Leadership Gut Check review meeting.

Leadership Accountability Peer Groups

Another extremely simple, yet powerful, practice involves meeting on a quarterly basis with a group of like-minded peers. These individuals may be fellow leaders in your current organization. They can also be individuals outside your organization. The key is that they are like you: fully committed to stepping up and being truly accountable in their roles.

These meetings involve six to eight leaders. They usually last sixty to ninety minutes. They can be conducted face-to-face if everyone is located in the same physical location, or they can be successfully conducted via telephone or video conference if your peers are in different geographic locations and time zones.

The meeting structure is very straightforward. One person volunteers to act as a facilitator. Some clients like to use our coaches as facilitators, but it's not critical to the success of these meetings. The facilitator's primary job is to guide the conversation and ensure everyone has an opportunity to participate. Here's a typical agenda for a

Regular Practices for Living the Leadership Contract

Leadership Accountability Peer Group ninety-minute meeting that is self-facilitated by a company's own leaders.

Welcome and Check-Ins (10 minutes). The meeting facilitator welcomes the group and invites everyone to provide a quick check-in describing how they are currently doing and feeling.

What's Worked Well in the Last Quarter (20 minutes). The facilitator asks participants to spend one minute sharing what has worked well in the past quarter in their leadership roles and to highlight specifically how they have stepped up in meaningful ways.

What We Are Struggling With (20 minutes). The facilitator then asks participants to spend two minutes sharing something they are currently struggling with in their leadership roles and where they want some help from the group. Typically, the items discussed involve the hard work of being a leader.

How We Get Stronger (30 minutes). The facilitator then shifts the focus on how the leaders can become stronger or how they can support one another with specific issues.

Check-Outs (10 minutes). The facilitator wraps up the meeting by asking each participant to do a one-minute check-out. The person can share how he or she is feeling after the meeting, share a personal commitment that they will focus on over the next quarter, or provide an offer of support to another member of the group. The facilitator for the next quarter's meeting is identified.

It has been fascinating to see these groups take hold within companies. For one client, we introduced the idea to the top 120 leaders during a leadership forum. This company was embarking on a significant leadership transformation. They wanted a way for leaders to support each other and build a great sense of community and a strong leadership culture.

When we shared the idea with the leaders, they all jumped at it. They formed fifteen groups of eight leaders each. We told them how they could structure their meetings using the agenda format above, and they did the rest. The client recently told me that the leaders are starting their third year of this practice. What an amazing result! Talk about stepping up and being accountable.

Many leaders have spontaneously set up these groups after attending The Leadership Contract leadership programs. Others have used the same strategy when they have participated in other development programs offered by their companies. It's a great way to sustain the learning while building a strong sense of community.

Here are a few other ideas to keep in mind as you set up your own peer group. First, these meetings should be focused strictly on discussing leadership accountability; they are not operational meetings or problem-solving sessions for business challenges. Set up other meetings to tackle those issues. Second, if the meetings start becoming gripe sessions where everyone spends time whining and complaining about the company, then stop the meetings immediately and reconvene when the group is ready to be truly accountable.

Groups have become fairly creative with these meetings. Some have used them as book clubs where the leaders all read the same book and devote part of their meeting to discussing the content and ideas. Other groups have created a spotlight component where one or two leaders are given extra time to discuss a challenge that they are facing and ask for insights and perspectives from the peer group. Another spotlight idea is to tackle a specific topic during the meeting. There are a lot of ways to make these meetings as meaningful as possible to you and your colleagues.

 Activity 9.3: Create Your Own Leadership Accountability Peer Group

 20 to 30 minutes to complete

Take a moment to think about the peers in your organization who would really be interested in working with you in a leadership accountability peer group. Write down their names. Identify how you will approach them and set up a group.

_____

_____

_____

The Leadership Gut Check Review Meeting

As I shared in *The Leadership Contract*, I believe that truly accountable leaders set aside some time each quarter to reflect on their leadership. Here are some questions that other leaders have used to guide their quarterly reviews. Try these out for yourself.

Activity 9.4: Questions to Guide Your Quarterly Leadership Gut Check Review

20 minutes to complete

How did you do as an accountable leader over the past three months?

_____

_____

_____

_____

What were some of the critical leadership decisions (Big D and small d) that you made?

_____

_____

_____

_____

What value did you bring to those you are obligated to?

_____

_____

_____

_____

_____

What hard work did you tackle? What hard work did you avoid?

_____

_____

_____

_____

_____

In what ways may you have allowed yourself to settle and possibly show up as a mediocre leader?

_____

_____

_____

_____

How did you strengthen the sense of community among the leaders in your organization?

_____

_____

_____

_____

Looking ahead to the next quarter, how will you continue to put the four terms of the Leadership Contract into action?

_____

_____

_____

An Annual Practice for Living the Four Terms of the Leadership Contract

I also believe it is important to invest some time annually to reflect more formally on your personal level of leadership accountability. Here are some ideas for you to consider for your own annual review:

- Redo The Leadership Contract Self-Assessment that I introduced in Chapter 2 to determine whether there are any gaps or areas for improvement.

- This is a great time to take out your personal leadership timeline and see whether there are meaningful experiences that you would add to it.

- Review your leadership obligation statement to see whether it still inspires you and is still relevant for you.

- Determine whether you are still tackling the hard work in your role.

- Identify the relationships with peers and colleagues that you know you have made stronger.

In Chapter 11 of *The Leadership Contract*, I also provide a set of questions (categorized under each of the four terms) that you can use as the basis of your review. You can also solicit feedback from some of your managers, direct reports, and peers with whom you work frequently.

In the next activity, you will be asked to identify the key questions that will be meaningful for you to include in your annual leadership gut check review.

Activity 9.5: Questions to Guide Your Annual Leadership Gut Check Review

10 to 15 minutes to complete

Review the section titled "Quarterly and Annual Actions" in Chapter 11 of *The Leadership Contract* book. Write down in the space below the questions that will be most valuable for you to use in your own annual leadership gut check review.

_____

_____

_____

_____

_____

_____

_____

Final Thoughts

Becoming a truly accountable leader takes discipline, effort, and attention. The good news is that by incorporating just a few of the simple practices discussed in this chapter into your own leadership role, you'll realize enormous benefits. I encourage you to come back to these ideas and modify them in a way that suits your own style and learning preferences.

The Turning Points of Leadership

This section consists of Chapter 10, which revisits the concepts of the turning points of leadership that I first shared in *The Leadership Contract*.

THE LEADERSHIP CONTRACT FIELD GUIDE
The Roadmap to Becoming a Truly Accountable Leader

SECTION ONE	SECTION TWO	SECTION THREE	SECTION FOUR
The Core Ideas	The Foundational Practices for Living the Leadership Contract	The Regular Practices for Living the Leadership Contract	The Turning Points of Leadership

⑩ Use the Turning Points of Leadership to Make Better Career Decisions
Make better career decisions and step up as an accountable leader when it matters most

Chapter 10: Use the Turning Points of Leadership to Make Better Career Decisions

This chapter shows you how to use the turning points to make better career decisions. It provides targeted insights and advice, depending on whether you are new to leadership, in a front-line or mid-level role, or entering the executive ranks.

Use the Turning Points of Leadership to Make Better Career Decisions

I n *The Leadership Contract*, I introduced the concept of the turning points of leadership, which represent moments in your career when what it means to be a leader changes significantly. I described four specific turning points (see Figure 10.1).

Each of these four turning points is important because the expectations, demands, and pressures you experience as a leader will increase considerably. As a result, you have to think about your role and understand what has changed and what will be expected of you. Unfortunately, my team and I have found that few leaders actually do pause and think about these changes.

Many become so excited about being promoted, taking on a more senior leader role, or thinking about the pay, perks, and power that they jump into the new role blindly. Then months later, they start to realize what that new role really demands.

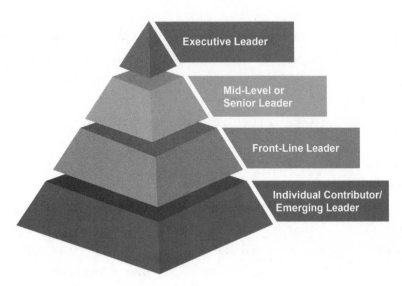

Figure 10.1 The Turning Points of Leadership

Many other leaders haven't necessarily jumped into a leadership role; they were backed into one. They were thrust into a role by their manager and didn't feel they could say no or were given little (if any) time to think about what they were signing up for.

When you do pause, even for a little while, you will find that the role you are considering signing up for will have many expectations and demands. You will find it will require you to shift your mindset and see yourself in a different way. You will realize that, to be successful in the role, you will have to be clear about what is expected of you and how you need to evolve in the way you lead to succeed. You can't just jump into a new leadership role full of naïve enthusiasm or assume it's just another career move. Instead, pause and make sure that you are clear about the changing demands and pressures of your new role. You must be certain you are truly prepared to live up to these demands to ensure that you will succeed when you take the leap.

This is exactly the focus of this chapter: to help you take charge of the career decisions you will make, and to be more deliberate when you take on a new leadership role. The activities in this chapter are targeted to each of the four turning points. This means you do not have to complete all of the activities; you can simply focus on the ones most appropriate for you. Below is some additional guidance on how to approach the activities in this chapter:

- **Your Current Leadership Role.** Chances are you have never really thought about the questions I'm going to ask you. As a result, a good starting point is to go to the turning point that corresponds to your current role and work through the activity. You will come away with greater clarity about your role. Many leaders state that they also end up recommitting to the Leadership Contract.

- **A Future Leadership Role.** If you are contemplating pursuing a more senior role in the future, then complete the activity for that corresponding turning point. For example, if you currently have a mid-level leadership role, but you want to secure an executive-level role in your company, then you may find it valuable to complete the activity for the executive-level role. It'll help you better understand the expectations, demands, and pressures of the executive-level role, which in turn will help you determine whether it is something you want to pursue.

Following, I list the specific activities for you to complete depending on where you are in your own leadership journey and the turning point that is relevant for you.

- Complete Activity 10.1 if you are aspiring to or are already in a role as an individual contributor and are being asked to step up as a leader.
- Complete Activity 10.2 if you are already a front-line leader or aspire to the role.
- Complete Activity 10.3 if you are in a mid-level leadership role or aspire to have one.
- Complete Activity 10.4 if you are in an executive-level role or are targeting your career to that level.

You will find that the reflection questions for each activity are the same, but since you'll be thinking about them from a different turning point, your answers will be very different.

Turning Point 1: Individual Contributors and Emerging Leaders

Many individuals in important individual contributor roles are being tapped on the shoulder and asked by their organizations to step up as leaders. In my experience, I find many of these individuals are often confused. Some may not think of themselves as leaders, but they need to start. Others do see themselves as leaders, but may be tentative because they have realized how complex and challenging it can be.

 Activity 10.1: Turning Point 1: Individual Contributors/Emerging Leaders and the Leadership Contract

 30 minutes to complete

Go to Chapter 10 in *The Leadership Contract* book and read the section on Turning Point 1. Answer the following questions:

Use the Turning Points of Leadership to Make Better Career Decisions

What is the leadership decision you need to make as an individual contributor or emerging leader?

_____

_____

How do you need to think differently about your leadership obligation?

_____

_____

_____

What is the specific hard work that you know you must tackle to be successful in your role?

_____

_____

_____

What key relationships with peers and colleagues will you need to rely on to help you be a more accountable leader?

_____

_____

_____

What specific expectations, demands, and pressures do you face in your role?

_____

_____

_____

What excites you about this role?

_____

_____

_____

Describe in detail what strong leadership accountability looks like at this turning point.

_____

_____

_____

_____

_____

_____

Use the Turning Points of Leadership to Make Better Career Decisions

Turning Point 2: Front-Line Leaders

Front-line leaders have some of the most critical leadership roles in companies today. The expectations, demands, and pressures are greater than ever before. As a front-line leader, it's important to fully appreciate how you need to show up as an accountable leader.

 Activity 10.2: Turning Point 2: Front-Line Leaders and the Leadership Contract

30 minutes to complete

Go to Chapter 10 in *The Leadership Contract* book and read the section on Turning Point 2. Answer the following questions:

What is the leadership decision you need to make as a front-line leader?

_____

_____

_____

How do you need to think differently about your leadership obligation?

_____

_____

_____

What is the specific hard work that you know you must tackle to be successful in your role?

_____

_____

_____

What key relationships with peers and colleagues will you need to rely on to help you be a more accountable leader?

_____

_____

_____

What specific expectations, demands, and pressures do you face in your role?

_____

_____

_____

What excites you about this role?

_____

_____

_____

Use the Turning Points of Leadership to Make Better Career Decisions

Describe in detail what strong leadership accountability looks like at this turning point.

_____

_____

_____

Turning Point 3: Mid-Level Leaders

I have always believed that mid-level leaders are the glue within any organization. Leaders at this level work on so many critical enterprise-wide projects. The expectations are many, and the demands are great.

Activity 10.3: Turning Point 3: Mid-Level Leaders and the Leadership Contract

30 minutes to complete

Go to Chapter 10 in *The Leadership Contract* book and read the section on Turning Point 3. Answer the following questions:

What is the leadership decision you need to make as a mid-level leader?

_____

_____

_____

How do you need to think differently about your leadership obligation?

_____

_____

_____

What is the specific hard work that you know you must tackle to be successful in your role?

_____

_____

_____

What key relationships with peers and colleagues will you need to rely on to help you be a more accountable leader?

_____

_____

_____

What specific expectations, demands, and pressures do you face in your role?

_____

_____

_____

Use the Turning Points of Leadership to Make Better Career Decisions

What excites you about this role?

_____

_____

_____

Describe in detail what strong leadership accountability looks like at this turning point.

_____

_____

_____

Turning Point 4: Executive Leaders

Executive-level roles are often the most coveted in any organization. The power and the prestige can be alluring. But these roles come with tremendous expectations and scrutiny. Not everyone is suited for this type of role. These roles require a high degree of personal accountability, resilience, and resolve.

 Activity 10.4: Turning Point 4: Executive Leaders and the Leadership Contract

 **30 minutes to complete**

Go to Chapter 10 in *The Leadership Contract* book and read the section on Turning Point 4. Answer the following questions:

What is the leadership decision you need to make as an executive-level leader?

_____

_____

_____

How do you need to think differently about your leadership obligation?

_____

_____

_____

What is the specific hard work that you know you must tackle to be successful in your role?

_____

_____

_____

What key relationships with peers and colleagues will you need to rely on to help you be a more accountable leader?

_____

_____

_____

What specific expectations, demands, and pressures do you face in your role?

_____

_____

_____

What excites you about this role?

_____

_____

_____

Describe in detail what strong leadership accountability looks like at this turning point.

_____

_____

_____

 ## Other Ways to Leverage the Turning Points of Leadership

Over the course of your career, you will find other opportunities or turning points where you'll need to make an important career decision. Next, I outline some examples and also share how to use the turning points with your own direct reports so that they can make better career decisions.

1. Saying No to a Leadership Role. Leaders tell me all the time that they feel tremendous pressure from their organizations to accept a leadership role once it is offered. I can personally relate to this. Early in my own career, the organization I worked with had an implicit rule: *If you were ever offered a leadership role, you had to jump at it because if you didn't you would never be given another chance.* I find fewer organizations are like this today, but many still send this message. So it's up to you to take control of your own career decisions. If after completing the activities in this field guide and in this chapter you feel you are not ready or suitable for a role, then you have to be honest with yourself and your organization. This requires courage and personal maturity. You must know what your unique value is (your leadership obligation) and how you can best contribute to the success of your company. It isn't always through a leadership role. If you love being an engineer and it's your passion, then be an engineer. If you love being an analyst and you are simply awesome at it, then be an analyst. Also remember that these are not one-time, permanent decisions. As your career evolves, you may change your mind and be ready to take on a leadership role at some point in the future.

2. Understand When You Are at Your Best as a Leader. The other important career decision is knowing when it's time to stay put. This means recognizing the level or turning point at which you particularly excel as a leader. Not everyone has the make-up to be a chief executive officer. Some people have just the right make-up to excel at the mid-level, for example. The world has changed today. All leadership roles are critical, and you can have significant impact on employees and your organization from any level. I believe it is important to know yourself well enough to fully appreciate where you add the most value as a leader. You don't necessarily have to climb the ladder to have a meaningful career and feel you are having an impact.

3. On-Boarding into a New Role. One of the most critical times in leaders' careers are when they on-board into a new leadership role, particularly when it's at a new turning point. If you are a leader in this situation, you must pay careful attention to this transition. You may find you experience a sense of loss related to what made you successful in the past. This means you must let go of what defined your past success because, in many ways, it's no longer relevant in your new role. You must begin to reach out to others for information and guidance. You also need a sense of who you can trust and what the agendas of others may be. It's also important to get a sense of your purpose and obligation as a leader and ensure you anchor your role to it.

4. Career Discussions with Your Direct Reports.   You can also use the activities in this chapter to work with your direct reports who aspire to more senior leadership roles. Have them complete the activities based on their desired role and level, and then have a career discussion with them. You will find that your direct reports will really value spending time with you. You'll also be able to share your own experiences (from your personal leadership story) and expectations to help them gain greater clarity and commitment.

Final Thoughts

Leaders at all levels must live up to increasingly high expectations. It's important to be clear on what those expectations are and how we need to step up as leaders. This chapter helped you gain insights so you can make more effective career decisions for yourself and help those you lead do the same.

Conclusion

Congratulations on reaching the final chapter of this field guide! I hope that the many ideas and activities have helped you think deeply about your leadership role and have given you specific ways to step up and be a more accountable leader.

As you will recall in the Introduction, I asked you to think about and respond to several questions. I also said I would come back to those questions at the end of this book. So here we are.

I would like you to read the questions below and write your answers. Please do not go back to your earlier responses. You'll have a chance to do that shortly. For now, just respond to the questions below.

 Activity C.1: Pause and Reflect on Your Current Leadership Role

 30 to 45 minutes to complete all activities in this section

Write your answers in the space provided for each of the following questions.

1. How would you now answer this question: What does it mean for you to be a leader today? Tomorrow?

_____

_____

_____

2. What has shaped you to be the leader you are today? How will you continue to evolve into the future?

_____

_____

_____

_____

_____

_____

3. What do you consider your primary obligation as a truly accountable leader going forward?

_____

_____

_____

_____

_____

_____

_____

4. In what ways is your success as a leader being impeded, and will continue to be impeded into the future, because you are avoiding some difficult things that you know you must do but haven't done?

_____

_____

_____

_____

5. To what extent do you have trusting and mutually supportive relationships with peers and colleagues at work? What more do you need to do going forward?

_____

_____

_____

_____

_____

_____

Activity C.2: Compare and Contrast Your Answers

Now go back to the questions you answered at the beginning of this book and compare them to the answers above.

What differences do you see?

_____

_____

_____

_____

_____

Where have you seen the greatest shifts in your thinking?

_____

_____

_____

_____

_____

_____

Do you sense a different tone in your responses now?

_____

_____

_____

_____

_____

 Reflections

When leaders compare and contrast their responses from the beginning of the field guide to the end, they see some striking differences. For many, their first responses are vague or unclear, with little to no conviction.

If you are like most leaders, you will find your answers above to be much more clear and direct. You will also sense a more decisive tone in your responses. This is a result of all the activities you have completed in this field guide. You have become a more deliberate leader.

Another pattern I see is that the earlier responses often lack inspiration. I bet that the answers above have more emotion to them. If you let someone else read your answers above, he or she will feel this emotion. The reader will be excited about the impact you intend to have as a leader. More importantly, you will be excited about your own leadership role.

Finally, the other shift we often find is directly tied to leadership accountability. The early responses were not convincing anyone that you were a truly accountable leader. I suspect that has all changed now. Everything about what and how you answered the questions above sends a strong signal that you are a truly accountable leader.

As I explained earlier in the field guide, these questions are ones I believe every single one of us in a leadership role needs to answer—not just once, but throughout our leadership careers.

The world in which we lead is more dynamic and complex than ever before. Organizations are facing unprecedented disruption, change, and transformation. Our world also faces complex societal problems. All of this places intense pressure and scrutiny on you and others in leadership roles.

Leadership matters now more than ever, and we need leaders in every facet of society to step up and be truly accountable. We need leaders who can lead transformational change, make their companies successful, and make our world a better place.

I believe that truly accountable leadership is the only way to build an organization that can not only survive in our increasingly complicated world, but also succeed and grow. Truly accountable leadership is the only way we can create vibrant countries and a secure society that will enable all people to lead meaningful lives.

As we have explored throughout this field guide, the first step is to understand you are being held to a higher standard of behavior when you take on a leadership role. Many leaders seem not to be fully aware of this. This is why the idea of a leadership contract is so important today. You need to understand that when you take on a leadership role you are signing up for something important. You can't just take on a role for the title, the perks, or the increased compensation. You need to pause and reflect on the four terms of the Leadership Contract:

- Leadership Is a Decision—Make It
- Leadership Is an Obligation—Step Up
- Leadership Is Hard Work—Get Tough
- Leadership Is a Community—Connect

Activity C.3: How Will You Step Up to Be a Truly Accountable Leader?

10 to 15 minutes to complete

Based on the activities you completed and the personal insights you have gained from this field guide, how will you now step up to be a truly accountable leader?

_____

_____

_____

_____

What will be the benefit to you? To the people you lead? To your organization?

_____

_____

_____

_____

_____

You see, when you internalize the four terms of the Leadership Contract and commit to being a truly accountable leader, you will experience many benefits:

- You will stand out as a role model for others because your decision to lead means you are setting the pace for other leaders. You will be the leader others want to emulate.

- You will bring greater value to your organization because you'll never lose sight of your leadership obligations. You'll be clear on the value you must create for your customers, employees, stakeholders, and the communities in which you do business.

- You will continually move your organization forward because you won't shy away from the hard work of leadership.

- You will have the courage, resilience, and resolve to take on the hard work because you'll know that if you don't no one else will. You will have the courage to have tough conversations.

- Finally, you'll be seen as a community builder. You'll commit to connecting with your colleagues across your organization. You'll help create a climate of high trust and mutual support. You will create a strong leadership culture that will become the ultimate differentiator.

Congratulations once again on the work you have done in this field guide. I wish you success in your leadership journey!

About the Author

Vince Molinaro, PhD, travels the world helping organizations successfully transform themselves by building strong leadership cultures with highly engaged and truly accountable leaders.

A *New York Times* best-selling author, speaker, and leadership adviser, Vince is the global managing director of the Lee Hecht Harrison Leadership Transformation Practice.

As a senior executive himself, Vince doesn't just preach leadership accountability—he lives it every day. His passion for strong leadership extends to his writing and global research. He is a go-to source for media, and his writing has been featured regularly in some of the world's leading business publications, including *The Harvard Business Review, Forbes, Inc.* magazine, and *The World Economic Forum.*

Vince's best-selling book, *The Leadership Contract* (Wiley, 2018), now in its third edition and available in several languages, is a must-read for all leaders. It currently serves as the foundation for culture change and leadership development at companies around the world. He's also the author of *The Leadership Contract Field Guide* (Wiley, 2018). Vince has also co-authored two other books: *Leadership Solutions* (Jossey-Bass, 2007) and *The Leadership Gap* (Wiley, 2005).

He believes that a company's ultimate differentiator comes from building a strong community of leaders and so he shares his weekly insights and best practices on leadership through his *Gut Check for Leaders* blog (www.theleadershipcontract.com). He can also be followed on Twitter @VinceMolinaro and Facebook.

Vince and his family live near Toronto, Canada.

Step Up, Get Tough, and Commit to Your Decision to Lead

The Leadership Contract provides the manual that leaders around the world need. With only seven percent of employees feeling confident in senior leadership, the problem is evident: disappointing and often *disgraceful* leaders. Employees deserve better than that; organiza-

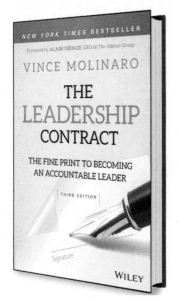

tions *need* better than that—and this book provides a robust framework for stepping up and making the decision to lead. This new third edition has been updated, featuring a new foreword by Adecco CEO Alain Dehaze, new findings from the Global Leadership Accountability Study, and more insights to help you chart your own path to build strong leadership accountability at a personal and organizational level.

Great leadership doesn't happen by accident. It's more than just being in charge; it's a decision, an obligation, and potentially your legacy. Mediocre is no longer good enough— in today's business climate, organizations need stellar leadership. If you're not exceptional, step up or step aside—this book helps you toughen up and put your commitment to great leadership in writing for *yourself* as much as everyone else.

- Learn how a leadership contract is vital for truly accountable leadership

- Discover the mindset and practices needed to be a deliberate and decisive leader

- Communicate to inspire, motivate, and drive high performance

- Become the leader your organization needs today and into the future

Leadership is not a birthright, not an accident, and not for everyone. It is the only differentiator between an organization's success and failure, and it has been entrusted to you. Can you step up to the challenge? Can you execute strategy while inspiring peak performance, nurturing top talent, managing complexity, creating value, conquering uncertainty, and yes, developing new leaders? Put your name on the line—literally—by drawing up a contract for leadership accountability. *The Leadership Contract* provides a proven and practical framework used by companies and leaders around the world. Join them and take your leadership to the next level.

Bring *The Leadership Contract* into Your Organization to Build Strong Leadership Accountability

We offer several solutions based on the powerful ideas in the best-selling book *The Leadership Contract: The Fine Print to Becoming an Accountable Leader* (third edition).

Keynote Presentations

Many companies have taken advantage of our thought-provoking and practical presentations to share the ideas in *The Leadership Contract* with their leaders as part of management retreats, leader forums, development programs, or kicking off large transformation initiatives.

Learning Programs

We offer a series of learning programs to help leaders step up and become truly accountable in their roles:

The Leadership Contract™ Seminars and Workshops. Our hands-on Leadership Contract seminars and workshops (instructor-led, virtual instructor-led, blended) transform how leaders think about their roles and shift their mindset of what it means to be a truly accountable leader.

The Accountable Manager™: A Front-Line Management Fundamentals Program. The Accountable Manager is a blended learning program for new or experienced front-line managers. This modular program (instructor-led, virtual instructor-led, blended) develops the core skills that front-line managers need to be successful, and helps them step up to their leadership accountabilities.

Leading from the Middle: Inspiring Accountability. This modular program (instructor-led, virtual instructor-led, blended learning with digital components, assessment and coaching) targets the specific capabilities that mid-level managers need to excel in their roles and helps them step up to drive real organizational impact.

Advancing the Development of Women in Leadership Roles. This program helps organizations address their diversity and inclusion priorities by specifically helping women accelerate their personal growth and development in their leadership roles.

The Leadership Contract for Teams. A powerful one-day classroom experience that translates the ideas from *The Leadership Contract* to build truly accountable teams.

The Leadership Contract for Human Resources Leaders. This program helps HR leaders and teams truly step up to help their organizations drive leadership transformation and build stronger accountability at all levels.

Consulting

We offer a series of services to help organizations build strong leadership accountability.

Leadership Accountability Audit. This solution is ideal for organizations that need greater insight into the state of leadership accountability at all levels. The insights from our audit become an important foundation to implement targeted solutions.

Leader Forum Design and Facilitation. We work with leading organizations to build strong leadership cultures among senior leaders by designing and facilitating dynamic meetings and off-sites.

About Lee Hecht Harrison

Lee Hecht Harrison helps companies transform their leaders and workforce so they can accelerate performance. In an era of continuous change, successfully transforming your workforce depends on how well companies and their people embrace, navigate, and lead change.

We bring our expertise in talent development and transition to deliver tailored solutions that help our clients ensure they have the people and culture they need to evolve and grow. We are passionate about making a difference in people's careers and building better leaders so our clients can build strong employer brands.

A division of The Adecco Group—the world's leading provider of workforce solutions—Lee Hecht Harrison's 4,000 colleagues work with more than 7,000 clients in more than sixty countries around the world. We have the local expertise, global infrastructure, and industry-leading technology and analytics required to manage the complexity associated with executing critical talent and workforce initiatives, while reducing brand and operational risk. It's why 60 percent of Fortune 500 companies choose to work with us.

LEE HECHT
HARRISON

About the Adecco Group

The Adecco Group is the world's leading provider of workforce solutions, transforming the world of work through talent and technology. Each year, The Adecco Group provides more than one million people around the world with career opportunities, guidance, and insights. Through its global brands Adecco, Modis, Badenoch & Clark, Spring Professional, Lee Hecht Harrison, and Pontoon, The Adecco Group offers total workforce solutions, including temporary staffing, permanent placement, career transition, talent development, and outsourcing. The Adecco Group partners with employers, candidates, colleagues, and governments, sharing its labor market expertise and insights to empower people, fuel economies, and enrich societies.

The Adecco Group is a Fortune Global 500 company, based in Zurich, Switzerland, with more than 33,000 FTE employees in sixty countries and territories around the world. Adecco Group AG is registered in Switzerland (ISIN: CH0012138605) and listed on the SIX Swiss Exchange (ADEN).

THE ADECCO GROUP

Acknowledgments

I want to begin by expressing my personal gratitude to my many clients around the world. Without your commitment to my work, none of what has been accomplished would have happened. I have been blessed with many deep and long-standing relationships over my career. I'm also grateful and indebted to those of you who brought the ideas of *The Leadership Contract* into your organizations. Our work with you became the foundation of the insights shared in this field guide. Thank you!

I want to also thank the many readers of my books and blogs. I deeply appreciate your support. I especially value when you have reached out to me to share how my ideas have helped you become a more accountable leader. It is personally gratifying to receive this feedback. I'm always thrilled to hear from leaders who have applied the ideas, and that has made them better.

I wish to acknowledge several colleagues. From the Adecco Group: Alain Dehaze, chief executive officer, Stephan Howeg, chief marketing and communications officer, and Shanthi Flynn, chief human resources office—thank you for your encouragement and support. From Lee Hecht Harrison: Peter Alcide, president and chief operating officer, Claudio Garcia, Chris Rice, Greg Simpson, Jim Concelman, Jeanne Schad, Beth Rizzotti, and Helene Cavalli. Your contributions have been many and deeply appreciated. A big thank you also to my many global colleagues and peers—your commitment to my work is deeply appreciated.

To my long-standing colleagues who have contributed their ideas and insights to the ideas in this field guide: Tammy Heermann, Dr. Alex Vincent, Tess Reimann, Joey Edwards, Dr. Seonaid Charlesworth, Dr. Liane Davey, Dr. Mehrdad Derayeh, Dr. Tracy Cocivera, Dan Lett, and Dr. Kim Rogers. Your commitment and passion are constant motivators for me. Many thanks to Adri Maisonet-Morales, Christine Tobias and Barbara Meens-Thistle for their suggestions and comments on the ideas in this book.

An extra special thank you to Razia Garda for your tireless efforts to keep me organized and productive—you are my secret weapon!

Thank you also to Dr. Nick Morgan, Nikki Smith-Morgan, Sarah Morgan, and Emma Wyatt of Public Words. Your full commitment to me and my ideas are deeply valued.

A big thank you goes to the team at John Wiley & Sons who contributed greatly to this project. A special thank you to Shannon Vargo, my editor for the past five years. Thanks also to Elizabeth Gildea, Chris Webb, Peter Knox, Dawn Kilgore, Pete Gaughan, and Kelly Martin.

Finally, I wish to acknowledge my family. To my children, Mateo, Tomas, and Alessia. I am proud of the young leaders you are becoming. To my wife, Elizabeth, for your unrelenting support. Nothing I do is possible without you. Thank you!

Index

Page references followed by *fig* indicate an illustrated figure.